HIGH
SCHOOL
STUDENTS
SPEAK OUT

HIGH
SCHOOL
STUDENTS
SPEAK OUT

BY DAVID MALLERY

A Study of the Impact of High
School Experiences on Students,
Conducted under the Auspices of
the Committee on School and Col-
lege Relations of the Educational
Records Bureau

HARPER & BROTHERS

PUBLISHERS   NEW YORK 16

HIGH SCHOOL STUDENTS SPEAK OUT
Copyright © 1962, by Educational Records Bureau
Printed in the United States of America

FIRST EDITION

B-M

Library of Congress catalog card number: 62-9913

TABLE OF CONTENTS

ACKNOWLEDGMENT

Although this study grew out of the cooperative effort of many persons—the members of the Committee on School and College Relations, the students, teachers, and administrators in eight secondary schools, the study director, and various consultants—it is primarily the product of the thinking, planning, leadership, and work of the former chairman of the committee, Dr. Burton P. Fowler. For those who have been associated with the study in any way, this point needs no iteration, but for those to whom this book is their first introduction to the study, I have been asked by Mr. Eldridge and the committee to state unequivocally that this study is very much Dr. Fowler's project in which they all are happy to have participated. This I gladly do, adding on behalf of the Educational Records Bureau our gratitude and congratulations to Dr. Fowler for his long period of productive leadership of the Committee on School and College Relations.

ARTHUR E. TRAXLER
Executive Director
Educational Records Bureau

FOREWORD

Unlike other professions, education is always beset with a conflict between purpose and performance. "Purpose" is an admirably suited topic for speech-making at graduation exercises or for the explosion of forewords. But few of the speeches or forewords ever flower into performance. The gap between learning in school and responsible social action, both in and out of school, remains to be bridged. The purposes of teachers and the purposes of learners are often miles apart.

In the study sponsored by our committee, we attempted to explore the values and frustrations of our high school students and the faculty concern about them. We hope to see established, where it is lacking, a frank and honest relationship between youth and adults. The teen-ager has his own cultural design, his own brand of sophistication. These often are not understood by his teachers. The teen-ager also has his own attitudes, motives, virtues, values, and social ideals. These need to be put to good use by teachers. Further, they need to find expression in high levels of behavior among teenagers. Until these two things occur widely, we are likely to mistake talk for behavior, structure for purposes, and conformity for maturity.

We may exhort to excellence but act with complacency. Listing uniform requirements and demanding harder homework make sense only if the ends are a love of learning and a respect for mature, responsible behavior. What is the status assigned to intellectual integrity and personal responsibility in the statements made in this report?

One high school senior says: "School is not a place to get educated in. It's a place to get you into college!"

And a teacher is quoted as saying:

> You know, a lot of times I think that these students would like it best if they were given a perfectly prepared, mimeographed course, with test questions and blanks for the answers, and a separate answer sheet from which to memorize the answers. And these are my brightest people. . . .

Yet, it is gratifying to find in this report the positive testimony of students quite free from cynicism. Here is an example:

xi

English is really the thing this year that is exciting. . . . We read things like *Death of a Salesman* and *Babbitt* and the kids really try to tie these things to themselves and their families and the community. It's terrific!

Never before has it been so important to discover and develop the rich resources of our high school population. The richest of these resources are vast and widespread capacities. They include more than high IQ's and debatable concepts of "talent." They include great potential for *creative* thinking and, quite as important, for *critical* thinking.

Let us not lose sight of the fact that creative and critical thinking happen in the mind of an individual. How characteristic it is of us in a time of emergency to meet a crisis with the panaceas of educational critics! Russian rigidity is a doubtful remedy for sick human relationships. Today our older boys and girls need friendly guidance rather than rigid rules and programs, more attention to the individual and his unique values, not less. Uniformity is the deadly virus of so-called democratic education. Because we need scientists, mathematicians, and linguists, there is no automatic reason for requiring all students to study science, mathematics, and foreign languages intensively. Nor should we set aside the arts. They are conspicuously minimized in most current studies of educational reform.

A great many teachers, students, and parents may find that this report will help them gain a better understanding of the high school's purposes and performance. Up to now too many of our professional educators have focused attention on academic progress without challenging students to action; on the critical need for change without stimulating students and teachers to respond to the need; on courses, units, mechanical devices, and hard work without stressing the importance of good citizenship.

The exchange of convictions and experiences found in this report should stimulate discussion in many forward-looking schools and communities that are trying to achieve a sensible balance in the midst of a Babel of voices. If we are to guide high school students toward higher standards of effort and achievement, if we are to expect such achievement to find expression in responsible action by teachers and students, then teachers and students must have respect for each other's convictions and concerns and must strive together for their realization.

BURTON P. FOWLER

PREFACE

What happens to a student *as a person* as he goes through an American high school today? What impact, if any, does the school have on his life and his thinking? These important questions have received little attention in the midst of the current controversy about the standards and goals of our educational system.

The Committee on School and College Relations of the Educational Records Bureau decided to look for answers through a field study of students in a sampling of high schools. David Mallery, a young English teacher at Germantown Friends School in Philadelphia, was appointed study director, and the project got under way in the fall of 1959.

In planning the project, the committee was able to profit from its experience in conducting an earlier study of college students[1] and from the findings of other campus surveys as reported by Eddy[2] and Jacob.[3] An interviewing procedure similar to the one used by Dr. Eddy was adopted, with the aim of getting students to reveal their feelings and thoughts freely.

The eight cooperating high schools, not to be identified by name, were drawn from the New England, Middle Atlantic, and Middle West regions. Here is a thumbnail description of them: (1) a denominational, coeducational boarding school in a country setting, enrolling 450 students; (2) a public academic high school in a large eastern city, with an enrollment of 1,600 girls, selected for high ability and character; (3) the corresponding public academic high school for boys in the same city, with an enrollment of about 2,100; (4) a public high school of nearly 1,000 students in a suburban community where the interest in college preparation is intense; (5) the comprehensive high school of a rapidly growing industrial town, enrolling 3,000 students; (6) a comprehensive urban high school with 5,000 students; (7) a rural school with 500 students, grades 7-12, drawn from eight surrounding communities; (8) a comprehensive high school of 1,800 students, situated in a medium-sized midwestern city.

[1] Agatha Townsend, *College Freshmen Speak Out.* New York: Harper & Brothers, 1956.
[2] Edward D. Eddy, Jr., *The College Influence on Student Character.* Washington, D. C.: American Council on Education, February, 1959.
[3] Philip E. Jacob, *Changing Values in College.* New York: Harper & Brothers, 1957.

During the first two days of his week-long visit to each school, the study director met with regular classroom groups, usually wtihout the presence of the teacher. He provoked the discussion by asking questions such as these:

"What are some of the things that have mattered most to you in your experience in this school?"

"What are some of the things that you think account for the changes in you between, say, three years ago and now?"

"What do you see as some of the real strengths of this school?"

He avoided stereotype terms such as "values" or "ethics" which might have prompted stereotyped responses. The students were encouraged to talk informally among themselves, rather than to direct all their remarks to the visitor.

The classroom visits were followed by interviews, always on a voluntary basis, with selected or random individuals or groups. Preference was given to group sessions with students of assorted types. Some meetings with teachers and guidance personnel were also included in the schedule. A personable high school senior boy accompanied the study director in a visit to one of the schools and assisted skillfully in the interviewing.

The report that follows took shape from the pattern of the students' statements and discussions, as viewed by the study director at the end of his visits. Six areas of major concern emerged from what the students said when they talked about the curriculum, reflected on teachers and teaching, reacted to the college admission crush, appealed for real responsibility, described the divisive forces working in their schools and communities, and, above all, evaluated the effects of their high school experience on their values and growth.

The seriousness and astuteness of the students who spoke is the most striking feature of this report. Their words reveal what is happening to them in their schools and may have far-reaching implications for schools across the nation.

It would be foolish, certainly, to let student opinions and desires form the limits of our nation's educational objectives. It would be equally foolish to ignore what students are saying about their high school experience and what they are becoming through it. Student motivation and convictions must have a place in our educational planning.

What the students interviewed in this study offer is not long-range perspective nor instructions on what to revise or conserve in the curriculum. They tell us about the experience of being in advanced chemistry, in the junior play, or in vocational English. On this, the experience of being a student in high school, they have something to say. It is these fragments of "what it is like to be here," which make up most of this book. Since our nation is in the midst of such a ferment about the goals of education and how to achieve them, these voices of several hundred high school students say something that should be heard, something that might add leavening to the ferment and make it more constructive.

HIGH
SCHOOL
STUDENTS
SPEAK OUT

PART ONE
The High School and Values

CHAPTER 1

GETTING VALUES OFF THE PLATFORM

We high school kids get pretty cynical. A lot of our values have been cracked. We're in a transitional period and we can't believe it all the way we used to. And one thing is for sure: our parents aren't our main influence any more. Sometimes it seems like a battle—us kids against our parents. The influences are going to come from some place else now.

This was a high school senior speaking, a boy near the top of his class in a big city public school. The eight boys and girls around him seemed to feel that he had stated their case well. These twelfth-graders were in the midst of an earnest, informal discussion in a little office the school used for mimeographing and filing. It was late in the afternoon and the rest of the building was quiet. The boy's firm statement—"The influences are going to come from some place else now"—struck home and brought me up short on just what my assignment was all about.

What are the influences that are coming "from some place else now?" Have schools any important part in these influences? What kind of experience does a boy like the one who was just speaking have, day after day, in his school? How is he touched by the current cry for more hard work and fixed requirements, experiments in television and programmed machine teaching, demands for ability grouping, and advanced placement? What experiences does he have as he goes through his four units of English, three of mathematics, and all the rest?

He has a collection of test scores to look at, numbers which point to some kinds of achievements and abilities and even qualities of personality. He has cards scattered about his attic recording a 92 in tenth-grade biology, an 86 in American history, and an "incomplete" in the winter term of junior-year physical education.

By listening to the public controversy on education and visiting his school, we can learn much about his educational setting. We find that

3

his school is reacting vigorously to this public controversy. For example, when this boy was in the eighth grade he took home very little work, while his younger brother who is now in the eighth grade takes home a startling collection of books and manuals each night. We learn that competition for marks is an increasing force in the school. We learn that his mother and some of her neighbors read articles that fill them with outrage about the foolishness of substituting driver-training and social dancing for Latin and algebra—though they have not seen a school where this has actually been done. We know about the controversy, the school schedule of courses and classes, and the numbers and scores that describe what is called the achievement of this boy.

THE STUDENT AND HIS OWN VALUES

What we do not know so well is what it is like to be a *person* in the midst of all this. Even the most vehement spokesman for a renewed attack on the three R's has a good word to say for what are usually called "values." "Citizenship" and "character" are used here and there, often with some embarrassment as if in apology for a lapse into sentimentality, but values are all right to talk about nearly everywhere. The only trouble with values is that they seem to dwell most comfortably on platforms. A distinguished teacher at Smith College, Elizabeth Drew, puts this nicely:

"Values" is another subject we hear a lot about now. "Values" seem to be rather vague entities which are always appearing on platforms in a lost or weakened or dying state; and there seems a general opinion that if we keep them there on the platforms long enough, and talk often enough about their state of debility and estrangement, they'll somehow perk up again and re-assert themselves in a healthy way. It doesn't seem to occur to people that "values" are not mysterious things lying around waiting to be revived by pep-talks: they are things created in our own individual consciousness from our own experience of living, and issue in our own actions.

The interviews quickly established a pattern for approaching the topic of "values." As one boy in the first school I visited said: "Watch out for bull questions. People will know the answers you want. And they'll either give them to you or they'll give the opposite, just for the hell of it." This warning came from a burly junior boy and it introduced me to one approach to the direct discussion of values. Right away I encountered guarded faces and wary comments at the mention of the word. Fortunately, the students in the schools were ready to talk about their adverse reactions to the sound of this word. I asked the boy and his classmates why they were reluctant to talk about values. Nearly every hand shot up and these were typical answers:

It's hard to talk about things like honesty and loyalty. Kids think you're sounding "Sunday school-y" if you do. Or the wrong people start talking about them in a way that is so drippy you feel you're ready to become a slob just to be different from their preaching.

We're not really cynical. A lot of the time we seem most cynical when we care the most. People are scared of being laughed at, caring so much that they'll get hurt. You'll find that when the chips are down the people will come through pretty well in this school. They don't talk like much, but there are times when they *do* pretty well!

ACTION BEYOND WORDS

The word "idealistic" was used with the same guarded attitude. Students often gave it an ironic connotation:

In your questions around here, watch out for the Idealistic Stuff. You won't know what those Big Idealists behave like, and it'll sound pretty good to you. You'll have to find out what they *do*. Come to us—we'll tell you!
I told them what I thought and they said, "Oh, you're just being idealistic!"
You got a pretty idealistic set of comments in that meeting today. What we *didn't* get to . . .
He's idealistic a lot of the time, but you have to admit he knows what he's doing.

Yet along with this attitude toward the word "idealistic," I saw in the students' *actions* many signs that they were far from pessimistic or cynical. The student apathy we hear about so often may be essentially a form of resistance to adult idioms about values. But resistance to verbalizations does not necessarily mean rejection of the precepts. I found much in the students' behavior that was heartening, because it was expressed in action rather than discussed as values.

The students' responses to such words as "values" and "idealistic" clearly indicated to me that the school's impact on these young people would be revealed best through their reports of *experiences* that they regarded especially important. The discussions would have to be focused on the experiences, allowing the implications to emerge unforced, if at all.

WAYS OF LAUNCHING THE DISCUSSIONS

Verbalizations were inadequate in other ways. Verbal opinions even on *issues* were not necessarily helpful in getting a picture of the school's impact on student values. Questions about H-bomb testing, at one extreme, or required hours of physical education, at the other, produced an exchange of words rather than revelation of convictions. Questions that intruded too sharply and too quickly ("Would you cheat on a mid-year examination?") had to be ruled out. So did questions about the brotherhood of man, the Golden Rule, or anything else suggesting the "Sunday school" pitfalls about which the first group of students had warned.

The most fruitful way of launching discussions in large classes was to ask the students to go straight to actual experiences in school and to talk about them. I avoided direct openings such as "What kind of challenge do you find in your history course?" or "How effective is your Student Council?"

One question proved to be particularly effective with some groups of students, though it puzzled some others. I would say, "Try to flash up in your mind the picture of yourself as you were in the middle of the ninth grade." Sometimes rippling laughter greeted the nostalgic image this evoked for the junior or senior. Sometimes confused faces met my request, and I would add, "Try to recall the concerns you had then, your ideas about friendship, the future, important things in school. . . ." Then I would say, "Now flash up a picture of yourself as you are right now." I would wait a moment, and again smiles would often greet the mental images. "Now, would you be willing to point to some of the things that have happened in high school which you think have strongly influenced the change from the ninth-grade version of you to the present one?"

From these rather general questions came sometimes a tentative hand in the air, sometimes a sudden burst of feeling, sometimes a careful, respectable "feeler" comment, or perhaps a controversial thrust to goad the surrounding students into action.

However the discussion began, it quickly led to a lively give-and-take. The students did not simply voice their opinions; they eagerly described their experiences, reactions, and discoveries.

Before plunging into the day-to-day experience of high school students, it seems appropriate to present first some of their personal insights. For it is in the setting of their changing views of themselves and the world that they are dealing with algebra, football, teachers, social prejudice, and the competition for college admission. Surely their new understandings and perplexities are worthy of attention.

This is all about what to ask kids & how to ask them!

CHAPTER 2

NEW UNDERSTANDING, NEW PERPLEXITIES

I think you get more introspective as you go through high school. Also, you look more critically at the world itself. I don't mean you decide you don't like the world. You just begin to examine the good and bad things in it, in your country, in your neighborhood—even in your school.

What this reflective senior girl was saying paralleled much that I had heard in the other schools about how the world looks to some young people. She went on:

It's easy to get cynical when you start seeing things more sharply, seeing the good and the bad. I think the advanced history people and the newspaper crowd get that way here. Some people decide they'd better stop questioning. Or they just settle for cynicism.

This girl was far from alone in wondering how she could profit most from the wider understandings she had gained as she moved through her high school years. Just where these wider understandings lead students is of crucial importance, for these new vistas bring with them new perplexities:

I think we have a hard time accepting religion any more at this stage. It seems to be taught like mythology—like Agamemnon or something—you talk to God and all. That seems so primitive. Yet maybe we aren't old enough yet for the *mystical* view of religion.

This was another recurrent theme: religion sometimes as a force to be opposed, sometimes as a mystery to be fathomed, sometimes as a goal to be attained.

Talk about these things came more often in individual conversations than in group sessions. In some schools—as one girl said—"People wouldn't be caught dead talking about this stuff!" In other schools, it seemed perfectly acceptable, exciting, actually *necessary* for people to

8

talk over these larger questions, though always outside of class. In still other schools, these questions seemed to "belong" in the school life. They were not relegated just to the lunch table or the recreation room.

In schools where "these things just aren't talked about," students were surprised at my interest, and spoke almost in a clandestine way about their widening understanding of social and religious questions, and about their own searching. Asked where such matters might be discussed, one girl answered, "I don't think other people think about these things much. Maybe it's just me." Yet a few minutes later, I would hear another student saying practically the same thing. To such boys and girls, the climate in one school seemed to rule out any sharing of this kind of thinking and questioning with one another.

There were other reasons for avoiding this kind of sharing. As one boy said:

> You can't resolve these questions—maybe ever. So you just cover up more and more—you cover up your disappointments or your ideals. You may get stung if you try to express them, or you may get into questions you can't manage.

One of his classmates, a girl, agreed and added: "You plunge into trivialities and try to avoid the big questions. At school you can just keep busy. There's lots to do. At home there's homework. The parents are no help. You start talking with them and they ask you if you have all your homework done or they make some big deal about what you're going to wear."

THE BIG QUESTIONS AND THE CLASSROOM

Most students seemed to feel that their attempts at self-examination and social criticism had to be kept private. Those who spoke to me about such attempts seemed to think their schoolmates were happy-go-lucky, insensitive, or just "had it made in life." They would say, "I seem to think this way. But nobody else does." In other schools, this kind of thinking appeared to be perfectly natural at any time, in any mood. A boy theatrically drawing up his chair at the lunch table might intone "Okay, let's talk about LIFE!" At the next table students might be arguing over baseball scores or fashions, and at another table students might be speculating on views of God, on cheating in biology class, or on "what was ethical."

Perhaps the appropriateness of students talking about ethical and philosophical matters is related to whether or not such matters ever appear as part of a school course or activity. It is hard to see how questions of moral and ethical standards, of belief and commitment, of *values,* can be kept out of a school curriculum that includes science, mathematics, language, social studies, literature, and composition, with all their implications. Yet apparently it *is* possible when the students are overwhelmed by a thousand activities, questions, answers, tests, projects, and grades. Somehow all these things simply drown the searching questions that might arise and might even be answered in a classroom. The students' vision of the relevance of a course can be obscured even when the teacher is quite conscious of the larger issues in his subject. But in a course where the teacher *himself* is lost in the minutiae of yesterday's exercises and tomorrow's corrections, what hope is there for students to reach into underlying values, questions, and answers?

Some schools see the issues which students raise in their own thinking as definitely "belonging" in certain courses. Students spoke up appreciatively for courses that introduced new questions which seemed worth exploring and answering. They seemed grateful for teachers who took the trouble to find out about student concerns and to bring these into the life of the school or to relate them to the actual work of a course. Thus students *and teachers* could sometimes, as one boy said, "talk about real life right out in the open."

INFLUENCES OUTSIDE OF CLASS

One effort to touch values in student behavior appeared in some schools' use of codes: codes of behavior, codes of honor, patterns for courtesy or sportsmanship. It was heartening to see certain students making an effort to bring these codes to bear on their actions. One girl spoke of her school's attempts to "get honor into the students' lives" by making them aware of the serious implications of academic cheating. This effort was described by a student honor committee as "realistic without being wishy-washy, strong without being rigid." Among the other students, the school's efforts evoked emotions that ranged from scorn to reverence. But once students had committed themselves to the code, a sense of real seriousness and purpose resulted. The teachers in this school seemed to feel that the honor code involved them as much as it did the students.

Whether the different kinds of codes have a personal impact on individual students or not, at least the codes invite a connection between noble words and everyday life in a school. These codes and honor systems, adequately implemented, can challenge students to put values into action.

In one of the schools—an independent boarding school—the students' comments clearly revealed that the religious commitment of the school had become an important and natural part of their lives. I met with the Religious Life Committee and found myself in the midst of preparations for a discussion program on capital punishment. In another group, students spoke of the impact of the Quaker meeting: for some, it was a time for sitting and thinking, even for rest; for others, it was more than this—whether or not they were members of the Society of Friends. One convincing piece of evidence of the impact of these Quaker meetings was that students readily remembered and described other students' comments, their "vocal ministry," in meetings of years gone by. In this school, thoughtful searching and sharing of experience was acceptable, actually part of the climate of student life.

THE SCHOOL, THE CLASS, THE PERSON

Two senior girls holding top elected leadership in their class were talking. One said:

We figure that our class once had three social strata. I'd call them the Untouchables, the Middle Group, and the Upper Echelon (the Nobility). At least this was the way I saw it in the tenth grade. And I know, because I spent time in each group.

Asked for the basis for the divisions, one girl answered, "Well, it was a matter of who went out with whom, what kids you cut classes with, what teachers you were rude to, things like that."

I picked up the idea of contrasting the tenth-grade picture with the present one, asking what caused the breakdown of the stratification. The quieter of the two girls answered:

I think it's that the two-bit idols started to collapse. They used to do things you wouldn't dare do—your parents would have killed you if you did them. But you used to admire the idols when *they* did those things. Then your admiration somehow wears off as you get older and these ex-idols seem a little pathetic if they keep doing that stuff as seniors.

The other girl took over: "It has something to do with college pressures —recommendations and all that."

"Yes," the second girl cut in, "and you see many a hypocrite working on that one!"

"Well, kids can't fool each other too well. They hate hypocrisy when they see it. The hypocritical kind pay a big price with the other kids, even if the teachers don't see what's happening at all."

Three boys and two girls, juniors and seniors, joined the group and quickly entered the conversation: "One thing about this change is that you have to live up to this idea of the-school-is-so-great." There was immediate argument about this.

"No, it isn't that. It's pride in *yourself* as a person that makes you value different people and different kinds of actions from what you did when you were younger."

"Yes, but that's part of the pride in the school, isn't it? You get that pride in yourself by being in a place that you think is worthy of pride."

This chance to look at their own development and that of their class as they went through high school seemed delightful to these students. This was true of a number of students in the different schools. Sometimes they spoke of a home room teacher, a subject teacher, a counselor, or a coach as someone who had helped them to see themselves as a developing group and as developing individuals.

I saw pieces of student writing in which a class's values were thoughtfully analyzed and traced through several years. In one case this was done in English classes and the work was read aloud by the writers. The essays were discussed hotly in and out of the English classes. One, entitled "My Class and I," began with the idea of conformity as a current national topic. Then it traced the kinds of conformity the writer had seen during the junior high school years in his own class. "In those days," he wrote, "the 'football men' established the social codes, the policy regarding students' relations to teachers, the unofficial listings of who was *in* and who was *out*." The eleventh-grade author classified himself under the social outcasts in the eighth grade. He described examples of cruelty and herd-mindedness he had observed from an isolated spot on the sidelines. This led to "an unhappy and insecure existence for almost everyone: the 'football men' who began to be tired of being followed in everything they did; the conformists who were constantly putting up a false front; and the non-conformists who helplessly condemned the others while being pushed around by them." Among the eighth-grade adventures he described were smoking in the basement, tormenting the class oddball, and developing systems of cheating on tests. The essay used these events to develop a picture of the class as it began to grow up and strike out for itself. Three weeks before he wrote his paper, the boy had been elected president of the senior class for the subsequent year.

Some of his classmates saw their own history somewhat differently. In their essays, they had described the experiences of the newcomer in the community, of the shy girl with a successful sister in the class above, of the boy all-out for athletics. They all read and discussed these essays in the English class, with the students divided into different groups in the room, each group charged with considering several essays carefully. The papers were studied and debated in the cafeteria and during recess time. The teacher's written notes on the papers dealt with standards of style, construction, and clarity. At the same time, he and the students seemed to assume that if the papers were worth writing, they were worth considering by members of the class. The careful preparation of the work, the intense listening and the thoughtful discussion, reflected something of the class's own maturing—its own efforts to solve its problems.

Here, at any rate, was sensible harmony of academic effort and thoughtful insight into certain human realities. The class was preparing for its senior year. Its future president finished his paper with this description of the present and future of his class:

Now the class is preparing for its senior year, the year of harmony and affection. Many of the past problems remain—the Hartville County girls still form a circle, and the old Misery-Loves-Company people are still together even though they are of different types and shouldn't always be together. Some still have the desire to hack. We are all responsible for this, but we are solving our problems. The men and women of the class have proved that maybe we're one of the best, not one of the worst, classes that have been here at school. I say men and women because I think we're grown up. We've worked together to solve our own problems and I think we shall continue to do so.

PART TWO
The Curriculum

CHAPTER 3

CURRICULUM IS CURRICULUM

Well, curriculum is curriculum. We have it for twelve years. We haven't mentioned it to you because we wanted to tell you first about the things that really matter.

The boy who said this was announcing what turned out to be one of the major themes in this study. He was surrounded by eight other boys from the three top classes in a high school. These boys, leaders of various student councils and activities, were meeting with me after most of the students and teachers had left the building. We had been talking for more than an hour about experiences that had "really mattered" to these boys. And nothing they had talked about had anything to do with what went on inside any classroom.

This happened in one of the first schools I visited. I had not yet learned to *wait* long enough. Instead, I asked with some curiosity: "What about some things in the curriculum? What has been especially significant there? This hasn't come up at all yet. How come?"

The boy's "curriculum is curriculum" seemed to say it all. The other boys nodded, and then took the conversation back to the things that "really mattered."

This idea, that school courses were a neutral element or even irrelevant in the pattern of things that really did have significance for high school people, was repeatedly expressed in the conversations in the schools. I ran into it in advanced college preparatory sections and among vocational students—in fast, middle, and slow groups. I heard so much on "curriculum is curriculum," and some of it was said so eloquently, that it deserves a key spot in this report. Courses that students said *did* have an impact, that did *matter*, seem all the more impressive in contrast.

Repeatedly the young people plunged into controversy or attack, or into celebration of certain courses, once the curriculum entered the

17

picture. Did a course make any sense? Was it worth doing for any reason other than to pass or get the "A"? Was it dead or alive—and in what way? In the fragments that follow, some of the students express the urgency they feel about the chance to think and work in a course as a whole human being.

"I haven't had a chance in any course to really think. They tell us you go to school to widen your understanding and all, but where are you supposed to do it?"

The boy speaking was in a classroom group of seniors in an academic course. There was a pattern of three or four hours of work a night for these seniors and tremendous competition for marks, national test scores, and admission to college. But no chance to think?

About fifteen junior and senior girls were gathered sociably in their recreation room. Their talk shifted to "the most important things that have happened around here." One girl tried to summarize her friends' comments about certain courses in this way:

"What we study in school seems so *unreal*. I have the feeling that what's real is 'out there.' We need bridges to 'out there.' " She made a gesture in the direction of the window.

Thirty-three vocational senior boys were gathered for an English class. The teacher tipped me off in advance that this was the brightest of the seven vocational sections. The boys were impressive and had plenty to say, including this comment from a quiet-spoken fellow who appeared to carry great weight with the others: "Last year we had a new shop teacher. He was right from industry! He was pretty rough and really put it to us. We were doing new stuff and hard stuff." The others joined in to explain the work in detail, and with real eagerness. Then the same boy spoke again:

Then other teachers criticized this fellow and the things we were doing. They said this work was too advanced for us, that we were using too expensive equipment. They said the shop kids weren't responsible enough to use this equipment. Anyway the work was stopped. They told the new teacher what was usually done, and we did it. It was back to stuff we had done before, over and over again. I was even back to making doors for cabinets. It was a real letdown. But the other was great while it lasted.

I was talking during a lunch hour with an attractive girl starting her eleventh-grade year. I asked what courses she had found especially valuable last year in the tenth grade. She said, "Well, I was in the advanced section in English—I liked being in that."

I asked: "What did you read in there that struck you as particularly interesting or worthwhile?"

"Well, let's see. We read *Paradise Lost* but that was pretty cut and dried. Then . . ." (she seemed to be reaching for some memory) "there was Shakespeare . . ." (her face seemed to cloud over) "but that was pretty hard to understand a lot of the time." She thought a moment more. "We *did* read some drama." She struggled to remember names of plays. Then: "We *did* have a free reading program that we got marked on. It wasn't the *number* of books we read, it was the *kind* of books, you know what I mean?"

Asked if there were any books that meant something special to her, she thought a moment, then answered, "Well, it's hard to remember." She smiled.

In some schools there were "wonderful exceptions," some classes that really mattered, where something significant did happen. In other schools such courses did not seem to be exceptions but expected and valued experiences. And sometimes there was a sudden flash of excitement in a course. One girl described such an event as she sat in what was ordinarily an English class. The students were hard at it in an earnest discussion about the courses that struck them as most important. A girl over at the side of the room raised her hand.

You know, in physics last week, it was really great. We got into a discussion of something, and we suddenly realized that there was no answer to the question we were talking about. We went on and talked about *possibilities*, about things we couldn't know yet, on the basis of the information we had now—and about things we needed to explore this century. And it was exciting to see that the teacher didn't know the answer—that he was talking about possibilities, about unknown regions, *with* us!

A boy I was talking with remained seated at the cafeteria table after the bell, trying to explain just what was so important to him about his history course:

History is the one course where you have the feeling that we're trying to see the whole thing—not just learn about pieces. Some days it's boring as anything. But it's only boring because we don't know enough to deal with the kind of questions he's asking. And we *know* that's what is the matter. But other days it really begins to take a shape. On those days the pieces add up to something, even if it's just new questions. And the past and present seem to go together, even though the way they go together seems to change as we go along.

"Could we talk some more?"

I recognized the boy from an earlier class discussion. He joined me and soon began to talk about the school and his own outlook on life, particularly about his serious, growing interest in international affairs. "I'd like to do something in international work," he said, and without mentioning any course, he went on to explain how this feeling had come to be important to him. As I listened to him, I recognized what might have happened in certain classrooms to contribute to this feeling:

. . . Then one night I put my finger on a map of Russia, and I suddenly thought that my finger was running across two hundred and ten million people—across people in their homes and on the street. It was the funniest feeling—as if I suddenly was connected with them—as if even there might be a Russian boy moving his finger across a map of the U.S.A. at this same moment!

"Have you visited tenth-grade math?"

"Have you met Mr. Hunter, the math teacher?"

"Do you know about this book we're working on in tenth grade?"

"I'm no math brain, but there's something really good going on in our tenth-grade math course. . . ."

I had been inside one school less than twenty minutes before this barrage of questions about Mr. Hunter and tenth-grade mathematics began. I soon found that Mr. Hunter was indeed working on a textbook and developing it with his students. The material was on mimeographed sheets, and teacher and students were testing problems, challenging each other on precise explanations, arguing over wording, and laboring over proofs and statements of principles. The students seemed to feel a proprietary interest in developing this book. Beyond this, it looked as if they were challenged by its special approach to mathematics. They seemed to see something of the design of mathematics and were trying to describe what they saw.

These students were clearly involved in the core of mathematics, not simply in a teacher's entertaining personality. "It sure is different from just pushing numbers around the way I always did before," as one boy said. These students were encountering mathematics material before it reached the textbook editors, curriculum makers, visual-aid committees, and the rest. They were not inventing something new. They were learning what had to be learned, but with a depth that made special sense. It looked like a creative partnership of the subject, the teacher, and the students, with each important to the other.

One girl was trying to put her finger on just what this experience meant to her, and she suddenly asked this question:

You know, I wonder if this year in math is an experience that will mean something just to us. Do you think once this book gets into final shape and is published and put into the hands of eleventh-graders, say, five years from now, that it will be the basis for dead, meaningless drudgery for them just as math books used to be for me before this year?

Mr. Hunter's tenth-grade mathematics class has something to say to us about students getting into a subject beneath the answer-giving surface. This type of penetration of a subject was happening for the boy who recalled the history course where they were "trying to see the whole thing." It was happening for a few minutes in the physics class, when the students and teacher got out of the workbook and into the unknowns of physics itself. And it was happening as the boy ran his finger over the map of Russia. Surely these experiences penetrated much deeper than did the "curriculum is curriculum" feeling, into something that genuinely did "matter."

CHAPTER 4

WHAT REALLY MATTERS

The school isn't supposed to influence you. It's where you do the assignment. It's just the intellectual side.

Most people around here figure that it's *the score you end up with that counts*. They figure that after you graduate the high school experience will seem pretty insignificant. So the big drive is on getting through at as high a level as you can. If some kid comes home with an "A" and you come home with a "D," you probably figure you have to do something about it—you can't just leave it that way. If somebody said to a group of kids that he'd just cheated in an exam, the others wouldn't look too surprised. They all know the drive to score and get out. And once you're out, it's the *getting through* and *how high the score was* that will count.

These are two contrasting views that I often heard on "what the curriculum has to do with what really matters." The first statement came from a girl in an advanced eleventh-grade social studies class. Her school was in an industrial community and offered academic, general, and vocational programs. The second statement came from a boy in an all-academic city high school. He was summarizing a fast-moving discussion for a group of advanced social studies students. These two views were recurrent, and they seem striking enough to warrant examination.

VIEW NO. 1: WHAT COUNTS IS OUTSIDE OF SCHOOL

I walked into the classroom and quickly saw a number of faces I had encountered two days before in an advanced English class. Since then I had been talking with vocational students, and I had some new concerns as I came into this room. It was an advanced class in social studies. I explained my project as quickly as I could for those students whom I hadn't met before, and then I tried a frontal approach to the impact of school on a person: "What would you say are some of the

22

major sources of influence on the kind of person you are?" Would anyone ask whether I meant in school or outside? No one did. At first many faces showed what looked to me like surprise, followed by serious thoughtfulness. Here is a brief sketch of the "sources of influence" these young people then described:

1. *Church.* Some said it affected "moral character," even the actual nature of one's personality. This brought some enthusiastic debate, though other students seemed rather uninterested.
2. *Home.* "That's almost everything."
3. *Friends.* "People you go around with."
4. *School.* They didn't get into specific aspects. They agreed to come back to all these general areas as soon as we had the main ones listed on the board.
5. *Entertainment.* "Movies, television, and reading."
6. *Travel.*
7. *Clubs.* "Scholastic clubs, fraternities, sororities, neighborhood groups, gangs." One girl said there weren't any gangs any more. Asked where they went, she quickly answered, "They went to jail!" There was a good laugh at this. Then several students explained there had been a problem of gangs but it was partly solved, both by "having a cop on every corner" and by the fact that "there got to be a lot more things for us to do around town."
8. *The city itself.* "Its opportunities, standards, activities."
9. *Your status.* "Your family's income." "Where you live." "The prestige of your father's job." These brought a tumult of argument on just how important such things were in shaping a person.
10. *Race.* "Relations and attitudes." They explained that the city had one "bad" area which was predominantly Negro, and this led to "some problems in thinking and values." There were no Negro students in the room.

When I asked if they could choose the over-riding influences from among these, *home* and *friends* got by far the most takers. *School* got none. When I asked for another major influence, still no one mentioned school.

Recognizing this, they set to work on the question of why *school* hadn't been considered to be one of the influences that affected their lives the most:

Maybe we just sort of assume the school's influence. We expect new ideas to come from there and don't think much about it.

I think that somewhere along the line one or two teachers have a terrific influence on you, even though the rest of the school may not have any special meaning.

School should be concerned with intelligence. It doesn't affect the personality. You have school, then you go home and enjoy life.

Maybe a very conscientious person would feel that school had influenced him a lot, but school isn't related to morals and those things. In school they give us facts.

One boy said vehemently: "The school shouldn't be concerned with moral and religious indoctrination. That's not its business." At this comment, a real concern took shape about the school's relation to what these students began calling "moral character." They were so anxious that the school not indoctrinate that they seemed to settle for a vision of school life as a rather irrelevant set of activities that one pursued before moving into other more important things.

Remember, these students were in the top-ability group in social studies in the eleventh grade. They "accepted" the business of school, did well in it, were generally pleased with it, but did not find it relevant to "what mattered" to them.

As far as I could see, these students were not under any special tension in competition for marks, national test scores, and college admissions. Was school irrelevant to them because their academic achievement was not important enough to their planning and motivation? Possibly, yet many vocational students in the same school felt that "if you're not C.P. (college preparatory), you're nothing around here."

VIEW NO. 2: WHAT COUNTS ARE MARKS

It was nearly twenty-five minutes after the end-of-school bell, but only one student had left the room. We had been hard at it throughout the last period and after the bell. These were also advanced social studies students, corresponding to the eleventh-grade group just de-scribed. In this school the lower limit of the IQ's was 110, and virtually all the students were college-bound. It was a big-city, aca-demic, public school. The drive on marks was the topic, and the intensity of the discussion accounted for the unnoticed clock and bell:

We're out for a real drive on marks—the city tests and the national tests, not just the school tests.

Yes, and we work this for all it's worth.

And so do the teachers!

You know, I sometimes wonder if it's really worth it, being in the ad-vanced course and getting all this terrific pressure.

Yes, you really have to convert yourself into a machine.

Well, you wouldn't, except for the school's neurotic obsession with college admissions and national tests.

Who's the school, though? Is it the teachers or is it us?

It's both. But we're in the fight and they know it, and they know they have us over a barrel.

The only way you can exist and actually grow as a human being in this set-up is to convert yourself into a machine—no, a *super*-machine—so that you can knock off all the work, hit the high marks, and have time left over to think and question and explore."

One boy turned to the boy who had just spoken and began to make machine-cranking gestures beside his head.

You know, we're really trained to be slipshod. Take this course. We know what kind of testing there will be. We do our reading for the teacher's pur-poses, not ours. We can chase through those chapters, pamphlets, and articles, and crack the test. We know how to do that by now. Yet it's possible that you might really get involved in the thing *for your own rea-sons* and then God knows what you might do on the test.

I guess the idea would be to be able to read for your own purposes AND for the teacher's, once you figured out what his purposes were. But it's easier to read just for the teacher's purposes—and the test's—they're the same. It's easier and it pays off.

You know, I got excited about something we were doing last fall, and I went to the library and got eight different books out on it and took them home. Two weeks later I took them back. I hadn't cracked one of them—I had been doing the regular homework the whole time. I wasn't even interested in the subject any more.

Outside reading! That's a laugh.

If we could even break out of this one-set-of-assignments lockstep. Most of us read the textbook four times to crack the tests. How about reading four textbooks once for the same test?

And finally, there came a kind of echo of some other concern, some remembered expectation: "But you still feel you're missing so much!"

These two groups of students had in common their age, their grade, and their well-above-average scholastic power. Yet their approaches to the curriculum were strikingly different. The first found "school" rather irrelevant to what really mattered to them. The second found "school" the crucial thing in their present lives. But "school" seemed to mean to the second group the techniques, rewards, and pressures of scoring high in aptitude and achievement tests. The common denominator was that *in neither group did anyone mention an academic course itself,* nor the ideas, materials, challenges, or processes of a subject. This is worth noticing at a time when hard work, ability-sectioning, and academic competition among bright students are so enthusiastically praised as goals in themselves. In these two classes, bright young people were cracking the school tests and some nationwide tests in their subjects. These were two advanced history sections. Both committed themselves on "what really mattered." Yet who was there to speak up for history's mysterious puzzles, its rush of events and their many interpretations, its personalities who, Tolstoy said, "were carrying on a work concealed from them but comprehensible to us?" "Modern history, like a deaf man, answers questions no one has asked." Who among these students had time or found it worthwhile to listen?

CHAPTER 5

"RESPECTABLE" COURSES

This course is the most awakening experience I've had in high school!

The boy speaking was enthusiastic, but I soon learned that the course he was talking about was to some students and some teachers not quite "respectable." This particular course was called Problems in Democracy, and the boy speaking obviously thought highly of it. A boy seated behind him supported him: "It's the kind of thing that makes you take a new look at the world around you."

Others tried to explain to me how much reading the class had done on city politics, issues in government, and local and national problems. Suddenly, one girl interrupted in a rather disdainful tone: "If you ask me, the course is a complete farce. You don't *learn* anything. I wish I'd stayed in French. They told me not to take the fourth year of French so I had to take *this* to fill out my schedule."

"What do you mean you don't *learn* anything?" the first boy asked, defensively.

"You don't get anything here you couldn't get from reading the papers closely. I can do that on my own if I want to."

"Do you?" he pressed her.

"No, but *that's* not the point."

"Well, it *is* the point, though. Did you know all these things we've studied about the city?"

They were not reaching each other. The boy and his supporters had found something "awakening" in this course that had made them look again at their city and their country. The girl and her supporters (all girls, interestingly enough) insisted that they "learned more" in French. The first girl was joined by another who was actually in fourth-year French.

"What do you mean, 'learn more'?" one of the boys asked her. "Do you mean you learn that something-or-other takes the subjunctive and where you put the *ne* and the *que?*"

The girl answered loftily, "We're not just studying what takes the subjunctive and that sort of thing. We study about Classicism and Romanticism." This seemed to impress some in the class, but one boy said, "What are those?"

The girl seemed totally stopped by that question. Perhaps she knew the English, even the French, words that are traditionally used to characterize Classicism and Romanticism, but she did not seem ready to say them, let alone explain them as something important in a country's literature and culture.

No doubt each of the two sides battling in this classroom had good grounds for their claims. It is possible that the Problems in Democracy course was too loosely organized and exploratory for someone who was more at home in assimilating information that had already been organized for him. It is also possible that the girls were speaking up for French because they had found it to be a respectable, memory-challenging activity rather than a genuine intellectual experience, as one might hope that advanced foreign language study could be. Yet it did look like a clear division between two attitudes about what was valuable in academic learning. Some of these students were convinced of the respectability of hard work in a learn-the-answer dimension. These people were insecure or hostile in courses where social problems and current issues were explored in a number of sources and in some complexity. Yet to the spokesmen for this "most awakening course," the experience itself counted heavily, "respectable" or not.

THE ARTS AND ACADEMIC RESPECTABILITY

I encountered impressive work in the arts in some of the schools. A good case could be made for the intellectual training and personal discipline that a tenth-grade boy was undergoing in the choir of one of the schools mastering the tenor part of Bach's *Magnificat*. The same could be true for the girl working on the alto part in Kurt Weill's *Down in the Valley* as she sat in the study hall. Such experiences in the field of music can have great value, involving concentration of mind and energy, sensitization and responsibility. Yet here again arises the question of Academic Respectability. How many students, like the worried senior I met, feel they should drop out of a chamber music group or an art major class or, in his case, the choir, because he "has to hit those subjects?" "After all, if I take that extra course, it'll look better for the college record." How many teachers would vote (as one drama coach reported they did in her school) to take a student out of a leading role in *Twelfth Night, The Hasty Heart, The Glass Menagerie,* or *Pygmalion* so that he could "get down to business"?

This is delicate ground. For, as one teacher said, "Students will kill themselves doing one thing and let everything else go. I can't compete with Joan of Arc in Spanish II."

What experiences in the arts really amount to something worthwhile in a school? The Community Sing and the Big Spring Show may pay off in developing cooperative social effort. But the area being considered now is serious, ambitious work in the arts, not Big Spring Shows. Teachers—and students—often confuse these two types of activities. Some of the work that passes for art, music, or drama in schools is surely of doubtful value, but the question is not just whether the performing arts should be included in the school program. It is whether having them done well is worthwhile. The boy who told me that playing the lead in *The Crucible* was the most important thing that had happened to him in school was not evading his academic responsibilities. His English teacher told me that "all the literary analysis in the world can't match what that play is doing for that kid as a person. And it's not so far from the kind of work he's learning to do in my class either." Yet, as one former choir member said glumly, "The experience won't give you any mileage in getting into college."

Young people can create myths of what is respectable, and what is not, just as devastatingly as teachers and parents can. How often are talented artists with high IQ's urged away from an art major and into an extra academic course because an adult or student-made aura of "dumbness" or "artiness" surrounds the choice of art? Maybe the student will feel safer in advanced French or mathematics. He rationalizes that he can "do the art on his own." And out goes one of his good opportunities for creativity, intellectual discipline, and real personal challenge. He is likely to become another casualty of academic respectability.

THE ADVANCED SECTION: MOST RESPECTABLE OF ALL

"You have to remember that we're in a regular class. But in the advanced classes they *do* think. I mean it's very different in there."

The girl spoke with no sign of irony in her voice. She was explaining to me that the "regular" classes have a rather dreary time of it. She was answering a boy in her class ("regular" eleventh-grade English) who had just said: "We just seem to do the homework, memorize, take tests, and get the marks. It's all just to get into college. I'd like some chance to think some in a course. Where is this big deal about education widening the horizons and challenging the mind about life and all that?"

To the girl, her faith that the students in the advanced classes "did think" and "were different" seemed a comfort. Another girl spoke up in support: "Yes, that's right. I was in the advanced section in tenth grade. People really talked about things. They connected the books to things that mattered—life—everything. Now here it's just the subject."

"Just the subject". As far as I could tell, this situation seemed perfectly natural to the students. Yet their school struck me as one big "advanced section." These classmates were high-powered and ambitious, and the performance in "regular" sections would seem "advanced" to many outsiders. I found this "regular" group lively, inquiring, and articulate. It seemed odd to save the exciting challenges for other groups when these students could profit so much from intellectual stimulation.

The same picture appeared in other schools. In one, I listened to a girl who sought me out to tell about the "tremendous experience" this year's work was for her:

English is really the thing this year that is exciting. I was in the regular section last year, but this year I am in the advanced section, and it is all the difference in the world. We read things like *Death of a Salesman* and *Babbitt*, and the kids really try to tie these things to what they see in themselves and their family and this community. It's terrific!

And in the same school, in a "regular" English class an hour later, one alert fellow was struggling to explain to the others some good points and values in *Silas Marner*. Others answered him while I tried to withdraw as much as I could from the front-and-center position in the room: "But the things we read in here have nothing to do with the present —with us. *Silas Marner, A Tale of Two Cities,* that essay book—it's all—distant!"

The first boy started in again, vainly, saying that "hot" issues "like conformity and keeping your integrity" were illustrated by *Silas Marner.* He was quite alone. But as he spoke, I thought of that girl and her "terrific" experience in advanced English. The regular section seemed to be crying out for what one girl called "something recognizable." And this was just what the advanced-English girl found so exciting in her study. It was the "something recognizable" that the regular class, except for its brightest boy, could *not* find. The brightest boy, who had been put in the regular section because of scheduling problems, was ironically the only one who could see or contrive some personal relevance in the section's "regular" project of the moment, *Silas Marner.*

Doubtless each of the teachers who was involved with the advanced section was understandably delighted with his pet project. And each could well be proud of the morale and the serious, enthusiastic attitude of the students in the advanced group. At the same time, these experiences seemed to lead these teachers into thinking that the "regulars" should not or could not deal with similar immediate, experimental, and meaningful challenges. The "regulars" themselves said they felt they were dealing with routine materials, flatly approached. "After all, we're just the *regular* classes."

A different picture took shape in a later afternoon talk with four senior boys and one girl in another school. The girl, a co-editor of the literary magazine, was a sprightly person whom the others listened to thoughtfully. One boy said:

You just work for marks and probably you get into college, and then you work to get into a good business or grad school, and then work some more for something. I wonder if there's ever a place where you really work to get some idea or understanding or just to *learn* something.

The girl did not answer him, but what she said somehow continued his thoughts:

You know, this year I got out of the honors English section. We were studying Elizabethan literature and I just couldn't care a thing about it, although everybody told me I was supposed to. I went back to this man, Martin, in a regular section. He'll sit back in his chair and raise a question like "Suppose you had every single thing—possession—that you desired but were all alone." We talked about that once, and soon we began to realize that we were talking both about the book we were studying and about our own city. He wanted us to think about this.

This girl had overcome the image of the "academically respectable courses" and had found something significant in Mr. Martin's course. Evidently the respectable courses in her school were the advanced courses in academic subjects, especially for students of her level of intellectual ability. Yet Mr. Martin's "regular" course had, for her, "respectability" in its relevance to her own experience and in its challenge to her own thinking.

CHAPTER 6
CURRICULUM, INTELLECT, AND SOCIAL STATUS

A girl will start thinking hard if she likes a boy and finds he's dumb and gets terrible marks!

A girl, whom I'll call Helen, was talking, and the subject that had her at loggerheads with two of her classmates was the relationship of a student's academic achievement to his social success. Previous studies of schools have reported extensively on the relation between academic and social standing. Some of the findings have supported the stereotype that the two are antagonistic, but readers sometimes forget the evident fact that enormous differences exist among schools and communities.

This particular high school was in a school- and college-minded suburban community. No vocational or commercial programs were offered. Only a few of the students were not headed for some kind of college. Helen and Betty were a striking and high-powered pair; Barbara seemed less articulate, but at odds with the school and anxious to talk about her view of its social picture. She was upset by Helen's words about the boy who is "dumb and gets terrible marks."

BARBARA (speaking up urgently): But couldn't he be good in something else?

HELEN: Well, you have to be *realistic!* What are you going to talk about all night?

BETTY: In some schools a girl has to play dumb to get boys. But here . . .

HELEN: If you want to go with dumb boys, you play dumb, of course. But around here that probably wouldn't come up. I think it's better to stay home— (she hesitated) for *a while*— (she laughed) than to go out with dumb boys!

BARBARA (struggling to get a word in): Well, I'm just not interested in school work. I like other things. (She laughed, then continued with some irony.) Maybe that's why I go out with jerks. Only they're really not jerks. They might look like jerks in this school. They don't go to this school, but there *are* other things besides academic subjects.

33

I broke in: Can someone who is poor in his studies get status here if he excels in some other part of school life?

BETTY: Maybe—say in dramatics. But a clunk couldn't get into a play. The deans would take him out so as to keep his time for his work.

BARBARA: That's not fair. Maybe he could really shine in dramatics. That might be the one place where he could reveal what he had on the ball.

HELEN: That might be true. The trouble is, if you're good in dramatics, you're probably good in other things too. You probably wouldn't have a good actor who couldn't write a sentence.

BARBARA: I'm interested in caring for animals. A boy could be interested in mechanics. This school doesn't touch these interests. If you have them, you're lost around here.

HELEN (thinking a minute, then summing up the situation): *It's just that those aren't the interests that are expected to take you places around here.*

In this school, Helen and Betty were clearly "at home"; Barbara was not. The much-discussed hostility toward the bright student was not evident here; some special problems apparently faced the slow student. The social prestige of academically successful people in this particular school did not seem to be simply a result of the community's wealth and concern for education. There are other schools where the college admissions pressure is intense and yet The Brain is rejected and must play dumb out of class.

At this school, Betty's and Helen's views seemed to be widely accepted by the other students. Few spoke up on Barbara's side. One real influence leading to the respect for bright people seemed to be the discussions and explorations of ideas going on in English and history classes. Students constantly referred to one or the other, usually English, with a special appreciation:

In English we get to discuss things that are on our minds, either in class or in the papers we write. You get to know people in a different way there.

I think the English teacher knows us better than anybody around here because she brings out our individuality more.

In history we work a lot on current world problems, seeing how they're related to the past. It's interesting, and you really get to *think.*

I saw another factor, possibly a cause for the prestige of the intellectually lively person, possibly a result of that prestige. This was that
virtually all the boys who were planning to major in engineering
wanted a liberal arts program with the engineering, even if it meant
an extra college year. Hardly any chose straight engineering training.
Apparently the students had found certain liberal arts courses at school
challenging and worthwhile, "even for engineers."

Here is an example of a curriculum with a strong influence, not because of a Social Conduct course, but because of experiences in certain
classes where students were challenged to think and speak as people
rather than as answer-givers. This was evident even from their casual
out-of-class conversations. In the newspaper office, three boys discussed
Crime and Punishment, Animal Farm, and *On the Beach* so heatedly
that the newspaper work was abandoned, and the session went on for
over an hour.

SOME CONTRASTS

In another school, I was talking about social status and intellectual
achievement with a roomful of junior girls. A number of comments
seemed to identify three of the fifteen girls as particularly alert and
academically successful. But they themselves seemed slightly defensive.
They spoke more softly than the others. They defended the idea of
intellectual adventure as a private, separate, satisfying thing for those
who wanted it. Their school was also college-minded, with most of the
graduates going on to some form of further education. Yet these students' feelings seemed different from Helen's and Betty's:

The super bright ones around here seem to go around together and stick
to themselves.

Maybe they just don't care about speaking to everyone or getting in with
the group.

Yes, but that doesn't mean the brightest people should be cut off from
the rest of us.

Maybe they find they are the only ones who can understand each other!

At this school, boys often spoke of the great emphasis placed on athletic success: "You can be a Merit Scholar and the girls will say, 'Gee, I wish I were bright enough to be a Merit Scholar!' But they go out with the football back!"

Nearly all of the leading athletes I met here felt at home and seemed to appreciate the general climate of the school. They seemed to be as much on top of things here as Helen and Betty had appeared to be in the other school. One possible reason for the difference in the social prestige of the intellectually successful person here and at the first school was that the courses seemed to be less exciting here. I listened for long periods of time without hearing any mention of the curriculum. Genuinely intellectual students may have found stimulus in the classroom or on their own, perhaps, by following up leads from the rigidly prescribed course work. But it seemed clear that most of the students were less "in action" and less challenged to think in their courses than was the case in the first school. Yet the volume of homework assigned and the get-into-college pressure seemed about the same in both.

Students in still a third school found the whole question of academic success and social prestige difficult to understand. There seemed to be no connection between the two. The academic side seemed to these students to be a project in itself, totally cut off from anything personal. Sometimes it was stimulating, sometimes not, but it was a world in itself. And when the academic side was discussed, it was usually in terms of marking practices, college admission standards, and teachers' attitudes toward students. The refrain about "people really coming into action" in the courses was absent.

These encounters raise a question worth considering: Can real challenge and excitement in the curriculum knock out vestiges of the old stereotype of the Rejected Brain, the Oddball Grind? Helen and Betty and many of their classmates spoke up often for the chances they had to think, to explore, to commit themselves fully in academic courses. Status usually comes from achievement in activities that are held in high esteem. If something personally challenging is happening in a class, the people responding to the challenge are likely to respect and value the experience and those who are most successful in it.

CHAPTER 7

SOMETHING BEYOND
THE LITTLE GREEN ESSAY BOOK

That discussion we had in English this morning was a big surprise to me. I never knew anyone in our class ever read Tolstoy, or Fitzgerald, or Stendhal! For that matter, I didn't know they read Kerouac and Spillane and all *those* either, though I sort of suspected that.

The girl who made this comment to me seemed delighted with her discovery. Her classmates' discussion of their own reading had been enthusiastic and intelligent. Yet apparently most of the courses were so centered on a textbook that such reading rarely came up for discussion in class or elsewhere. I had asked, "What are some of the things you have read during the last year which seemed particularly valuable to you?" "Valuable" was left undefined. I thought the actual or implicit meanings the students gave to it would be interesting to see.

THE TWO LISTS

From groups of students who did a good deal of reading, two lists of books emerged again and again. The first was usually an impressive collection, each title offered with enthusiasm, with almost a proprietary interest. Dostoyevsky, Faulkner, Hemingway, and Freud came most often on the "first list," with some respectable best sellers interspersed. Then a "second list" would announce itself, usually by a muffled laugh in some corner. I tried to listen carefully enough and watch faces so as to be able to associate a whispered title with the laugh or smile. When I did hear a title, I would simply write it on the board beside the other titles. *Return to Peyton Place* or two or three of Jack Kerouac's books would appear in my hasty scrawl beside *Anna Karenina* or *The Wall*. This often produced more surprise. There were expressions that seemed to say, "Those titles should not be there on the same board—they don't belong with the kind of books mentioned in school, even on a period off like this."

But what surprised me most was the company in this second list. Once it was "all right" to mention that someone—or everyone—had read *Return to Peyton Place,* the second list would come pouring out. Sometimes a student would offer apologetically *A Farewell to Arms* or *The Catcher in the Rye* among the *"Peyton Places."* I would ask, "How come you seem to apologize for these?" The answers: "Well, they're about things that wouldn't *go* around school," or "They're *current* books—I mean this century. I mean they aren't the kind that would *last* or anything," or "That's not a *teacher's* kind of book."

It seemed clear in more than one case that these statements were supposed to apply both to *On the Road* and *A Farewell to Arms.*

Sometimes there was relief all around that the books on the board could include such a range of titles. Sometimes the same boy or girl mentioned a book by Tolstoy and a book by Mickey Spillane. Other times, the students seemed to be confused to find that the "second list" had appeared. When this happened, illuminating argument developed about just what constituted "trash." One boy made an eloquent statement for the experience he got out of reading *Hot Rod.* The others seemed to respect him for this. The class also responded favorably to another boy's quick and thoughtful comment on what *The Brothers Karamazov* "had given me."

The disheartening thing about these conversations was that so often the students were surprised that such discussions occurred at all. A typical comment was: "In school we never get to talk about what we read on our own." The girl who was so surprised at her classmates' reading said both "lists" startled her. I asked her what things everybody read in English class. She answered, "Oh, you know, the usual—a green essay book, *David Copperfield, Idylls of the King*—those things."

The fact that many thoughtful students did high-powered reading on their own was impressive. It was unfortunate, though, that this reading seemed to be cut off from the school curriculum—even from English and history courses. One is led to wonder how these students managed to develop sophisticated discrimination in their reading habits. Did the stimulus for intellectual exploration come from sources within the school setting or from their families and friends?

Perhaps the most unfortunate students are those whose school courses have never stimulated in them any desire to read or explore. How many school libraries are used mainly to house students in unassigned periods? How many stand virtually empty all day long while librarians paste, clean, organize, and whisper? Are there many schools where the final bell brings three or four students into the library to browse, but sends some hundreds or thousands of others straight home? Are there many public libraries which are deserted unless mass high school assignments threaten them? One community librarian spoke of seeing forty students come in at the same time to read one of two assigned books, one written by William Dean Howells and the other by Sarah Orne Jewett. "More liberal teachers may give their students a list of *five* choices," she added with some discouragement.

At least the students who composed the two book lists were reading eagerly and making serious demands on their reading experience. In other groups, including some college preparatory classes, only a few current novels were mentioned by a few people, or the whole idea of reading on one's own simply fell flat. How often do actual courses have anything to do with individual reading exploration, either to enrich it, to make use of it, or, when necessary, to get it launched at all?

I encountered some courses that did stimulate reading interests. One was a vocational English section where the students were invited to take some initiative and delight in reading. The class included some able, intellectually curious youngsters and others who were limited in reading ability and verbal power. Yet the teachers gave enough enticements in the actual course work to succeed in getting the students to do a lot of reading and individual follow-up work on their own. A visitor might question the presence of a number of copies of *Captain from Castile* and the *Saturday Evening Post* in the room. But this was an approach to an individual reading program which resulted in increased use of the rather meager library. All the boys seemed to be developing considerable interest in reading, even those with unfavorable home backgrounds. This stress on individual reading was in the actual course, not a hoped-for extra on the outside.

I found a college preparatory course in which students were expected to read on their own and were asked to keep records to show the teacher at specified times. "He doesn't count the books or weigh them to see how heavy they are," one girl said. "He just wants us to know that he expects us to read, and he seems interested in knowing what we're reading." This class hooted at one boy's comment about his former school:

The books were piled up on the shelf with a big Book Report Card in each one. You were supposed to fill out this IBM-deal card as you read the book. But who wants to read a book and make a puzzle out of it? If he wanted us to read, he had to require it. He wanted it both ways—"voluntary" and with detailed, deadly reports.

In contrast, here in the boy's new school, students wrote papers bringing together different ideas from what they were reading, and they carried their reading into class discussions of works the group had read in common. As one boy said, ". . . We feel that there's some place for the things we're each interested in, even though we study a number of things together."

Another boy spoke up: "You figure if a teacher gives you some room for the things *you* care about, then you'll go along and give a break to the things *he* cares about."

A girl warned, "But you have to have time for the things you do on your own. Some teachers tell you to go to work on outside reading, and then they fill up the *inside* so much that you can't even finish *that*."

"THAT'S OURS—DON'T KILL IT BY PUTTING IT IN THE CURRICULUM!"

This warning was given by a girl in an all-academic public school. She and four students from regular and advanced sections were sitting with me in a corner of the empty school library. They had been talking eagerly about Camus's *The Plague*, Dostoyevsky's *Notes from Underground*, Swift's *Gulliver's Travels*, Freud's *Interpretation of Dreams*, and Fromm's *Escape from Freedom*. I asked if these were discussed in any particular course. They answered almost in chorus: "Oh no! That would kill them. *Everybody* doesn't have to be doing the same thing!"

Another joined in: "And everyone doesn't have to *cover* everything either."

Another added, "You make them part of the curriculum and you kill them. Then it's the old lock step. You're reading for tests, for the teacher's interpretation, for grinding analysis of point after point. They ought to leave us something that's *ours*."

I was impressed enough with this idea to try it out upstairs with a class, an advanced English class of seniors. They came forward with titles of books they had read independently. One boy spoke up after about six titles had been offered: "I'd like to know when you read these!" One answer came: "I was reading *Gentlemen's Agreement* until three this morning." They were off:

"That's a trashy item."

"Maybe it is, but it sure didn't put me to sleep."

"When were these others read? Joe, when did you read *East of Eden?*"

"Last summer."

"And you, when did you read *Crime and Punishment?*"

"Two summers ago."

"And Bert—how about *Of Mice and Men?*"

"Last week."

Apparently in a spurt of interest or defiance of the hours of home-work assigned, some of them would toss off a short book which gave what one girl called "an immediate pay-back," such as *Of Mice and Men* or *Gentlemen's Agreement*. The longer or more difficult books were not read at all unless time could be found for them during the summer.

"When are we supposed to read anything on our own? I'd like to read this *Doctor Zhivago*—but when am I supposed to do it? One night off from homework and I look like a clown in class and someone tells me my college chances are slipping!"

They laughed at the idea of "outside" reading.

If it's "outside," that means you don't do it. If it's assigned, then every-body does it.

Of course, there's assigned outside reading. Our class has ten weeks to read *Moby Dick* and *Barchester Towers* and write a paper on them. That is supposed to be *outside*.

Here were thoughtful, able people, eager for independent exploration in reading. Yet even they seemed startled at the next question I put to them:

"How would it be if each of you selected two major works of literature, making a deal with the teacher on which ones, and wrote your own paper on the two you had chosen?"

The idea seemed to appeal to them instantly. Then: "But then the teacher couldn't compare the papers fairly. How would he mark them?"

I seemed to hear the echo of the boy's words about the lock step.

WHAT STUDENTS EXPECT FROM THE CURRICULUM

Implicit in many of the quotations in these chapters are a number of complaints about the curriculum as it now is, and a number of clues as to what the curriculum might become if these complaints were answered. What guides to action do these young people furnish?

Let us look first at the negative side. At present these students find that their courses, for the most part, are too rigid, too heavily structured, and too remote from life, and that they are non-intellectual and impersonal. Professional educators could enter rejoinders or rebuttals to many of these findings. They could point out, for instance, that some of the young people ignore the need for focused, intensive work for the mastery which any valuable course involves. At any rate, the students show no awareness of this need as a goal in itself. Moreover, those asking for more loosely organized, exploratory activities are confronted by others who respond better to more logically structured courses and more clearcut goals.

A warning should be issued at this point. The groups in schools and communities that are also criticizing the curriculum should note that the students' demands go far beyond the stereotyped line often expected of them: to "make it interesting." A number of students talked about the heavy work load they were carrying. But their criticism dealt, not with hours and effort, but with the quality of thinking and motivation, which was lacking and which would be necessary to make the work load worthwhile to them.

A positive side of the challenge to the curriculum emerges clearly. Many students value and seek a personal involvement with their work; they want to be challenged, not just to be busier and struggle harder,

but to come to grips with ideas, experiences, and processes that seem
to have some relevance to them as human beings, alive right now.

Some of the students in this study are already working in courses
which are thoroughly engrossing. These courses are a practical demon-
stration of the answer to the girl who said, "That's ours—don't kill it
by putting it in the curriculum." They are courses where students are
given some responsibility for working out a program for themselves beyond the everybody-does-it minimum. There are other programs that
give a student something to do that is *his,* not just a teacher's pet project
or a test hurdle. These courses ask (and get) hard, concentrated effort
from the boys and girls. They are courses where teacher, subject, and
student meet. From the meeting something happens that "matters" in
intellectual training, in personal development, in social awareness.
With such a challenge, the high school does not have to mean what it
does to the student who said:

"All the learning I have been doing these three years has been outside
of school. This year especially there have been some real revelations.
But none of them have had anything to do with what we did day in
and day out in school!"

PART THREE
Teachers and Teaching

JOAN?

CHAPTER 8

THE ENCOUNTER WITH A TEACHER

. . . The really influential teachers around here have a lot of status with the students. They are the teachers who seem to get into our thinking. The students influence each other in things like what clothes to wear and how to comb your hair and all that. But these teachers seem to be in on the big things.

The seventeen-year-old girl who made this statement was one of many high school people I met who jumped eagerly to give examples of the constructive and important impact teachers can have. Few other topics evoked the force and enthusiasm that students showed in talking about teachers and teaching. These young people put great stress on "the teacher's personality" when they were praising a job of teaching.

"The teacher makes the course" is such a cliché that I hesitate to repeat it. Yet some version of this statement appeared many times as the students stressed that an outstanding teacher was an experience in himself, quite apart from his subject. *The experience with the subject* consistently took second place to *the encounter with the teacher.* Curriculum makers, textbook authors, publishers, and teachers themselves might feel the same jolt that I did when I heard students point to fine teaching as *transcending* the subject rather than *illuminating* it.

Perhaps such statements were made because these students—and their world—are so personality-conscious that in the classroom a *person* gets through to them with far more force than do principles, facts, processes, and ideas. One student said:

The most important thing around here is a teacher's personality—its interplay with ours—his ideas—the way he gets us to think—the way he shows his interest in us. . . .

This student, like many others, does suggest many facets of meaning for "personality." Other comments dealing with a teacher's personality also extended a good way beyond any usual definition:

47

Mr. Sullivan in music—there's a marvelous man. He teaches us about life. I've got a whole new set of standards for myself because of being in his choir!

Miss Mahoney will stop and talk about things. Sometimes it's philosophical or it's about the way people behave. But it's interesting, you know what I mean. With some teachers it would be horrible—a real bore. But with her, it's good.

Many students expressed touching gratefulness for the teacher who seemed "human" and emanated warmth. Several times we discussed whether students would choose a stimulating teacher or stimulating subject matter if they were faced with the choice. Almost every time the choice would be the stimulating teacher:

Miss Carlson could get you excited about the dullest subject!

I have a math class—it's really something. The teacher once wanted to be a psychiatrist. I think he's a teacher because he likes people. He's really an interesting guy. It doesn't matter that he teaches math, particularly. Whatever he was teaching would be interesting.

I know a teacher who could take the best book ever written and kill it dead as a doornail in one class period!

There was almost pathetic insistence, especially from the younger students, that they would welcome *any* effort from the teacher to put some life into the barren landscape of "just the subject." It often seemed as if "the subject" were an inert, dead thing which the right teacher could bring to life, or sometimes could encourage students to bring to life.

I was wary about discussing teachers at all, for fear of opening the door to personal griping. I particularly did not like the idea of getting into personalities, since the schools I visited were going so far to welcome me and to further this study and its concerns. Thus, I was all the more relieved to see how the students tended to focus on constructive comment. And they were almost always willing, on their initiative or mine, to move into a discussion of teaching as well as of teachers. Most impressive of all, they did this in a spirit of careful thought and analysis, rather than carping or idolizing.

CHAPTER 9

THE WAY A TEACHER TEACHES

Sometimes I don't go for this teacher-drawing-the-students-out bit. You feel he knows all the answers and is just keeping quiet to get them from you. You're just being maneuvered!

This comment came in the middle of a heated session in which students were arguing with each other over the value of class discussion in a course. There were many views on this, and on other ways of teaching, as these fragments show:

A teacher should give you confidence that you can do it.

A teacher ought to *explain*—he should come half way to the student.

No, he shouldn't. Out in the world nobody comes halfway. We've got to go the whole way.

I think it's exciting when the teacher puts things to you and suddenly you discover something about them that he didn't say. Then it's *yours*. You know it in a different way!

I like the student-to-student discussion better than the teacher drawing out the student. There is more freedom—you don't have to stick to the teacher's questions.

We waste a lot of time in discussion. I wish the teacher would just cut it out and give it to us straight. It would save a lot of time.

I get pretty lost when the teacher lectures. Like in science and mathematics, even though they're my best subjects. We talk more in English. You feel it matters more, as if you were important to the learning—as if your way of seeing things counted.

We try to have discussions now and then, but you make a thirty-second comment and the teacher gives a ten-minute development of it!

There's a teacher here who really gets the kids thinking. He pretends to

49

be against everything—student council, school issues, international issues. He gets kids to write and talk about these things, to dig into them, and get hold of them. He's kind of a Bernard Shaw type man. . . .

We like a course well organized, so you know what you're doing and so you can see how you get your marks.

I think there are three kinds of teachers: (1) the kind that teach the subject—really get it into you; (2) the kind that really make it interesting —tie it up with something you know about, seem to want you to care about it; and (3) the kind that put it in front of you—they don't care whether you get it or not—just put it on the blackboard and say "Good luck!"

Statements like these illustrated the many concepts of a student's role, from a passive group member to an actively participating individual. They also made interesting assumptions about the curriculum. The students hoping for the teacher to "make it interesting" talked about needing some life in a dull venture. Others wanted recognition for a valid opinion, or even a stupid one. Still others asked for a chance to take off beyond the limits of the teacher's question, or even of his vision.

Being recognized as a person by the teacher was deeply valued. In fact, it seemed fundamental to many a student's whole motivation in school:

I always used to think of school as a mechanical duty. You get up, get in the bus, go to classes—all by the clock. Then I saw that there were some teachers who really did have a personal interest in the students. This really hit me hard.

This need for recognition was one of many concerns about the conduct of classes. One group of forty, a mixture of college-bound and general students, was exploring these matters. "What's really tough is when there can only be one opinion in the room, and that's the teacher's. You have to accept it," one boy began. Other hands shot up. I noted fragments like these on the board to refer to as we went on:

This course is not open to people's opinions. If you give an opinion that seems out of line, he'll say, "Get a transfer!" [There was a big laugh from the class on this.]

Yes, and a lot of history doesn't have true and false answers. There are a whole lot of sides to some things. It burns you up to have to arrive at some neat little opinion on something and even *that* is announced by the teacher.

And sometimes when something does suddenly develop and a discussion seems to be breaking out, a teacher will cut it off because he's afraid we'll corner him or something. So he just drops the discussion by saying we're off the subject.

There was real anxiety about the way many teachers cut off talk that promised to challenge and awaken students to some subtler aspect of the subject. One girl described these familiar ways of closing a discussion as the "two killers": "That's off the subject" or "We haven't time to go into that." Evidently the "two killers" had cut off many interesting classroom discussions for these students, since they gave vent to feelings of intense frustration when this topic came up. The basic problem seems to be: How can students and teachers bring something challenging and explorative into the classroom and still avoid irrelevance? Students often felt that the *real* issue arose from varying concepts of "irrelevancy."

CONTROL: TWO MEANINGS

Sometimes "control of discussion" is confused with "control of class behavior." Most students seemed to agree with the girl who said, "You need a teacher who can control the class." Asked what kind of "control" she meant, the girl explained: "I mean control so there isn't some joker rolling pennies in the back of the room and somebody else muttering cracks and getting laughs."

I asked, "Are the teachers who have that kind of control usually the same teachers who have 'control' in the sense that you said earlier you *didn't* like—control over discussion along rigid question-and-answer lines?" The students seemed strongly agreed that these were two separate kinds of "control" and that there was no necessary connection.

A STUDENT'S OWN QUEST

How free is the high school student to explore the things he feels are really important? This question came up even more frequently when we talked about teaching than it did when we discussed the curriculum.

In one school a boy was talking about the kind of philosophical questions that seemed really significant to him in his own thinking: "Well, does God exist? Is His will inflicted on us or can we choose? Things like that." Asked if this kind of thing came up in his current courses, he replied:

No, and *last* of all in history, where we're studying different religions. The teacher lectures, or writes on the board. It is pretty much facts. There was a whole section on our personal religious questions and needs, but he thought up the questions and gave them to us mimeographed with sub-headings and all, with a title on the sheet: *Religious Concerns of Young People*. He said he wanted to bring it right down to us. But those questions were his, not ours. He never asked us what ours were. He hardly asked us what we thought of his!

Asked where students did talk about these things, if not in any courses, he answered: "Well, not around here at school. You know—people might say, 'Whaddya mean, you believe *that?*' and make fun of you or miss the point, so you figure you'll just stay off those things."

A similar problem was revealed in this girl's statement about a human relations course: "It's mostly lectures—it's pretty good. We had a sociologist—a wonderful man—and we had a psychiatrist as a visiting lecturer, too."

When I asked if students raised the questions which were on their minds in these sessions, she said: "Well, no. They were mostly lectures, and they were pretty formal. We appreciated them, but the speakers couldn't know what we needed to hear unless they knew *us* a little. And they had to just come and speak and then leave."

One group of students, many of whom were in an advanced history section, pointed out the need for allowing, even encouraging, mutual exploration:

We have the feeling that the teacher thinks he must always know the answer; otherwise he will look bad to the students.

I wish he could know how happy we would be to explore, to argue out possibilities, that it's no criticism of him if he doesn't know *the* answer.

It's pretty deadening to have to stay inside the parts of history, even within the parts of the book, where there is a single right answer—and one that the teacher knows.

I know a teacher who solves this problem before it comes up. He just walks in, sits down, looks at the textbook, and asks for recitations, one after the other. At least *we're* able to try to widen things out some!

If he could just see that his status with us doesn't depend on having the answer before he asks the question!

CLASS VISIT NO. 1: PAGES AND ARMOR-BEARERS

A brief picture of two classes in two different schools will serve to illustrate different kinds of teaching in action. These classes provide some dramatic contrasts, set against the background of the student discussion indicated above. The first was an advanced college preparatory English class. I had met with many of the same students the day before and had been impressed by their maturity and insight as they looked at their school experiences. The class was studying a scene from a play of Shakespeare. The teacher asked questions about the sequence of ideas in a speech. Some students were confused about what had been said. The teacher reproved them, urging them to study the scene more carefully. Then they started in on meanings of certain technical Elizabethan terms. Questions and answers followed on the difference between a "page" and an "armor-bearer." The students looked inept, uninterested. The teacher appeared to be disappointed in them.

CLASS VISIT NO. 2: NO TREES, NO TRACTORS

The second visit was to a class of students of limited ability. They took part in a so-called "modified" social studies section. The class was working on the westward expansion era in American history. The students looked appallingly inert and apathetic at the start. The teacher, a young man of about twenty-eight, got out a packet of black-and-white pictures, each about one-foot square, and started to hold them up for the class to see. His questions were based on the pictures, which showed plains areas, men building houses, wagons moving, flatboats floating on rivers, and interiors of houses. The pictures were faded and too small. But by a continuing flow of practical questions, the teacher

got the class more and more into conversation on just what physical conditions were involved in "going West." Every question demanded that
the students think out or imagine what kinds of ingenuity and effort
the situation required.

"What do they have to do now?"

"Then how are they going to build a house?"

"How do you think they'll go after food?"

Each question might invite a standard, automatic answer which
would not work in the context. The boy who rather indifferently said
they could build houses out of trees had to look at the picture again to
see that there *were* no trees. The girl who said, "They need a tractor,"
had to stop and try to imagine what they would do since they had no
tractors.

This kind of questioning might seem flat at first hearing. But soon
what was happening came out clearly: an awakening of curiosity and
enterprise in the students, and a gradual growth of enthusiasm in the
teacher's questioning and in his handling of the responses. He did not
let a single "verbalism" go by without pressing for clear explanation.

Questions especially appropriate to girls were directed at groups of
girls or individual girls, and the same with boys. Literally everyone in
the class either volunteered or was called on in a natural, unthreatening
way with a question to bring him in and challenge his interest.

These students seemed to be really *thinking*. Faces and bodies,
raised hands, and rising inflections indicated this. It was thrilling to see
the efforts they made toward identifying themselves imaginatively with
America's pioneers and toward meeting realistically the challenges to
endurance and ingenuity that those people faced.

A teacher of an advanced college preparatory history section might be
covering the same era, and he might be able to stimulate far more
impressive *verbal* performance. But would he actually involve more
thinking and understanding of the events as a human experience?

The teacher of this "modified" class talked to me afterwards about
his aims:

A class period like that is hard work. But it is rewarding, too. Those
kids feel pretty dumb and are pretty much puzzled by what goes on in
school. Yet, we can't just brush them aside as being unable to think about

American history. There are things they *can* understand and think out. And we can't just settle for giving them words to push around which they can't tie to anything they know.

He made one final remark which revealed a certain problem and one way of meeting it. This was after I had told him how his skillful, thrusting questions seemed to alert the students to real thought.

"Well, you work out that kind of thing partly in self-defense, too, you know. If you went in there and just quizzed them on the words in a textbook, you would probably have everyone asleep or in a riot."

A TEACHER'S OPINIONS

Students repeatedly made distinctions among several kinds of teachers. There is the one who has the courage and enterprise to offer his own opinions in contributing to a discussion. Then, there is the one who forces his personal opinion on a class and calls it The Right Answer. Even more frustrating than the latter is the opinion-less, anonymous figure, who just asks questions. Whether or not the students agreed with the opinions of the teachers, they appreciated knowing what the opinions were, and having them offered, not as truth, but as the teacher's current thinking, for use in any way the students saw fit.

One thing really is good, and that is that some of the teachers really have opinions. You know, they aren't just neutral; they really believe something and will argue and be just as strong-minded as the students.

Teachers' opinions revealed through implications evidently startled or amused the students at times. Take the case of the girl who said:

No, we don't discuss religion much or have too many talks on that kind of thing. It always ends up with people getting a little peeved and they never change their mind. One thing I'll never forget is when Miss X, who always puts her foot in her mouth, came into class and said, 'When I come in here I leave my religion outside and discuss the truth!'

A HUMAN ENCOUNTER

Many boys and girls talked about their appreciation of some teachers' personal awareness of *them*, outside the line of duty. Also, they seemed to value any chance to see teachers outside *their* professional roles. This kind of comment is worth listening to in the midst of our current problems with numbers of students, shortages of teachers, and experiments in mass teaching:

In our school the students respect the teachers because they get to know them a little outside of class. And the reverse works, too—they get to respect us. They say there are a lot of kids with high IQ's here. But it's not just that. The teachers respect what a person can *do*.

You'd never cheat in a test when you knew the teacher personally. Where the cheating comes in is when the students don't know the teacher or don't respect him.

You really get to know a lot of teachers here. You eat with some of them, they coach you, they're on the committees. You can see them outside the classroom. They're willing to work on a committee or a team with a fellow who looks pretty poor in their classes.

The English teachers around here seem to know most about you. They probably get it from your writing. Sometimes you can choose the ideas or subjects you want to write on and that is good, because you can figure out what you think, and the teacher can see what your thinking is like.

The best thing about this school is the way the teachers expect so much of us. They seem to have confidence in us and really want us to come through. You'd feel pretty bad letting them down!

CHAPTER 10

MR. SMITH AND THE SHOP KIDS

Those C.P. kids get away with anything. The teachers play along with them. If we pulled some of the things they did, we'd get jumped all over.

The boy was in a vocational English class, his school was in an industrial community, and "those C.P. kids" were the college preparatory students in the same school. This vocational section had been colorfully sketched by the principal as he and I stood outside the classrooom door. "Now you're going to see how the other half lives! Oh, they won't throw you out or anything. It's just that they're a pretty rough group." Their regular teacher also wanted to brace me for an ordeal before leaving me. "This is the *worst* group. Now tomorrow at 12:30. . . ." But my visit had all been arranged.

"There are twenty-two of them. One is in jail now in New York, a few others have been in and out of trouble with the law here in town. But they're good boys—you know what I mean? And they'll cooperate with you. But they may give it to you in a language you're not used to. They've been around." He had one final whispered word before turning to introduce me to the group and leaving the room: "Remember, these are the lowest IQ group and the toughest of the shop people. Tomorrow at 12:30 you'll get the highest group."

The boys went through courteous, rather formal comments in answer to my opening question about their view of the strongest and the weakest aspects of their school. One by one each boy rose to speak, and the others listened carefully. Then that one boy's comment about "the C.P. kids" swung the discussion into action. Another joined in: "Yeah, you don't have a chance if you're not C.P."

Then with a rush of feeling, they showed eagerness to talk about a real problem:

Somebody roars down the street with no muffler on his car and the teachers'll say, "There go those shop boys!"

In class they tell us we're lazy and dumb.

We have this physics teacher. It turns out you need algebra to do physics. We haven't had it. And he says he knows we haven't had it but we're too dumb to learn it, so we just go ahead with the physics!

I asked them about their mathematics—what they had already had—and one went on: "We've been having the same math now since eighth grade. You don't feel like doing much when you know you've had it before and you know you'll have it again."

When I asked how many would really like to tackle some more advanced work in mathematics, nearly every boy in the room raised his hand. There seemed to be a real respect for and awe of mathematics, and a sense that *here* was something they should at least be given a chance to try.

"We're still doing fractions. I did them in sixth grade. And they wonder why we don't look lively in there!"

They sounded genuinely bitter for a few moments:

We're supposed to be young adults. Teachers should try treating us like young adults and not like kids. It burns you up.

I don't think a teacher ought to swear at you.

They say we come to waste time, us shop kids.

You ask a question and what do you get? "Five points off for you, kid!"

You ask for help and you're stupid. You don't ask for help and you "don't want to learn."

The period was nearly over and I was anxious not to leave these boys in the middle of such a negative, even if heartfelt, discussion. I asked, pointing to the clock, if they would be willing to put in a final word for some experience in their school life which really seemed important and valuable to them. They thought carefully. Then one tall boy in the back rose.

"I had an English teacher last year, and he made you feel like a man as soon as you entered the room."

Others joined in:

"Yeah, he never called you 'hey kid' or yelled at you. When you'd say 'sir' to him, he'd say 'sir' right back to you."

"They talk about respecting teachers. Here was a guy where it went both ways."

Another, seeing the clock's hand approaching bell time tried to bring the ideas together this way:

"I think the best thing here at the school is the really sincere ones—teachers—who go all the way to understand the kids and give them a break."

The bell rang right after his last word. The boys sat still, waiting, it seemed, to be excused. I thanked them, and the whole group converged on the front desk to impress one crucial, suddenly important message on me:

That English teacher's name is Mr. Smith. Be sure to visit his English class.

That Mr. Smith, you go see his class. Come when we meet him tomorrow. We didn't say it very well, but you'll see.

Several boys quickly sketched a diagram of how I could find Mr. Smith's room, and they wrote down the time for his class. The boy who had volunteered to copy my blackboard notes of the discussion's main points handed me his note sheet as he left. The notes were in capital letters, neatly written. In large letters at the end, with three underlinings, he had written: VISIT MR. SMITH'S ENGLISH CLASS. ROOM 321, 7th PERIOD.

A teacher who did not discriminate against "shop boys," one who "made you feel like a man when you walked into the room," seemed more important to these boys, as the final point to be stressed, than their anger about what seemed to be discrimination against vocational students.

MR. SMITH IN ACTION

The next day's visit to Mr. Smith's class showed precisely what the boys meant about this teacher's sincerity and his respect for them. It also showed in action a man skilled in human relations and interested in his students. I could see the things they had appreciated: his light touch, his calling students by name, his way of combining encouragement with dignified expectation that they could do the work. This classroom work in English during time away from the shop, *could* be a strong influence on these boys' powers of thought and expression, even on their own values. Perhaps one of the best ways to destroy any social-outcast stigma attached to non-college preparatory students is to have fine teachers meeting with them in their academic *and* vocational work, supporting them, challenging them, and helping them develop their values, standards, and abilities to the fullest. Here was a man who could do the job.

Mr. Smith's personal achievement with his students seemed even more spectacular to me in view of my impression of the day's lesson. Here was a clear contrast between teacher and curriculum. The boys were using a workbook called something like "English Errors," and dealing mechanically with "*lie* and *lay*," "*raise* and *rise*," as if these were unknown Latin verbs. Words like "*transitive*" and "*intransitive*" were used to explain which forms to use. The sentences in the workbook would have been puzzling to Lord Chesterfield. But the teacher conducted the class with the mastery of a combined artist, football coach, and orchestra director, and the boys enjoyed the process. I could see this by their faces, their way of sitting, their whole response. I myself found the actual *exercises* almost impossible to handle. I am convinced that people do not think this way about language: seeing the setting for a word and then inserting the right form because of a rule on the board. But the boys in this section, presumably limited in what they could do with words and in their hopes for "English," were trying hard to learn the game.

Here was an effective and perceptive teacher, working with responsive, well-motivated students. Their needs in language study and their unusual maturity of understanding could have been met and used in an instructive, valuable way. The actual curricular material got in the way.

What emerged here is a picture of a remarkable relationship between teacher and students, in spite of a serious problem in group reputation ("those shop kids") which these boys felt in the school, and also in spite of course materials of doubtful usefulness for *any* student. I was glad I had seen Mr. Smith. His approach to his students as individual human beings was impressive and valuable. "Didn't we tell you?" one of the boys whispered to me proudly as he gathered his books together to leave the room.

CHAPTER 11

WOULD I BE A TEACHER?

You know, sometimes we find that maybe, for a minute we're thinking of actually being a teacher. This passes pretty quickly, of course, but still we get the feeling—every once in a while—probably because of some teacher we admired. . . .

When this study began, I did not plan to delve into students' attitudes toward teaching as a vocational goal. But early in my visits, I sensed that students have a strong tendency to share whatever joy of learning their teachers display or, conversely, to absorb any perfunctory or unsympathetic attitude they sensed in the teachers. Students seem to want to feel that they are a part of their school, which includes adults as well as associates. That they want to know their teachers is implicit in many of the statements they made about teachers' personalities and teaching methods. Students reject some teachers and accept others, but they are rarely neutral. In reacting to their teachers' traits, students get to know and evaluate the teaching profession as well.

I never asked "Would you consider being a teacher?" Yet the subject came up again and again, and with a dramatic variety in attitudes that showed how these school people *saw* the teaching profession.

MONEY

Many boys dismissed the possibility of becoming a teacher on purely financial grounds. As one senior said, "Well, I guess none of us would want to be a teacher. I mean, sometimes you look at a teacher and you see him drive a beat-up old car, and maybe his clothes aren't so nice, and you figure what the hell!"

A number of able, personable boys described the financial picture as a block to considering teaching as a career, no matter how much they might have felt drawn to it for other reasons. And whatever misconceptions they might have had about business and industry, they seemed sure of their image of the teacher's fate:

If you're going to college, you can choose between being a teacher, say, and an engineer. A teacher gets poor pay and an engineer gets good pay. People figure you might as well get the benefit of the college education and go after good pay.

I was interested in being a teacher once, I really was. But when I saw the money they made and the chance to get ahead that they didn't have, I gave up the idea in a hurry. I mean, in business or industry, the more you know and the better you are, the more rewarded you are. That isn't true in teaching. There ought to be some compensation for the amount of work you do and for how good you get.

The country needs good teachers, I admit. But who wants to go into teaching and get that pay? If you have anything on the ball, you want to go into things that pay better—medicine, law, engineering. So that leaves the second-stringers and the also-rans for teaching.

DISCOURAGING EXAMPLES

More boys than girls talked about the problem of a teacher's salary. But both pointed to other reasons for throwing out the idea of being a teacher. Some of them were discussing influences on their career choices. Suddenly one boy spoke up: "I was influenced. Do you know what did it? Seeing lazy teachers. You see a teacher with his feet up on the desk—too lazy even to get up and talk to you. That has an influence."

Others spoke of the teacher's appalling work load:

Who wants to live like that? They're in here at 8:15. The bell rings at 3:00, and they're off to the second job at 3:01. At night they're reading papers or planning lessons. They don't have any life. They're too busy to get to know any of the kids they are supposed to like enough to keep them teaching.

THE ARID CURRICULUM

To some bright and independent students, the high school curriculum seemed devoid of either human or intellectual adventure. Students with that attitude would hardly leap to the idea of returning to the high school curriculum *as they had encountered it,* to struggle with it from the other side of the desk. Even the image of themselves as potential curriculum makers in school systems was hard for some of them to take seriously:

You remember yesterday when we were talking about being in key supervisory jobs in the city school system? I think we all felt a little contempt for that sort of thing. They spell out the curriculum all nicely and neatly, and it sounds so good. Yet it isn't good by the time it gets into the classroom. And maybe the trouble is that it *shouldn't* be so darned carefully spelled out if the teachers themselves are on the ball.

HORROR STEREOTYPES

Some students who thought their own school experience was stimulating still shuddered at the general public image of "blackboard jungles." To some, this image appeared more real than the schools they knew firsthand. One boy who described himself as "really in action" in the life of his own school said this about a teaching career: "Who would want to even try to keep order by brute force in a roomful of people who don't want to learn in the first place?"

TEACHING AS A SIDE ISSUE

One position appeared a number of times in advanced sections. Both boys and girls criticized indifference or preoccupation on the part of their own high school teachers. Still, the students would make statements such as, "I would be willing to teach in a university graduate school. But for me the teaching would be a means to an end. You have to keep alive, so I'd teach. But I'd be interested in the *end,* which would be first the degree and then research."

Notice the implications of this next girl's statement with regard to teaching, and its contribution to the world:

You could do a lot of teaching in a graduate school, but on the outside you could really do something that would help all mankind. You wouldn't be just grinding out something over and over, year after year.

GOING AHEAD OR GOING BACK?

One troublesome idea that worked against any favorable view of a teaching career seemed to be that toward the end of high school many students think of teaching as *a return to the life they are just finishing.* Leaving high school stands for entry into The World, a real growing up. At this stage in their lives, planning to become a high school teacher may look like a rejection of this new freedom, a step back from the door into The World.

This same feeling may bring some dubious candidates to the profession. A student who is successful in school and feels at home there may choose a teaching career simply in the hope of continuing this pleasant, unthreatening style of life. Perhaps it is significant that several statements like this were made by girls rather than boys:

It's wonderful here—I mean the building, the atmosphere, the kids that make up the school. I'd like to come back here and teach some day.

Perhaps here is a kernel of a suggestion of a constructive way of attracting capable people to the teaching profession. If young people find their school experience rewarding, admire their teachers, feel involved in something purposeful rather than in dreary routine and arid busywork, then they may see the profession as attractive in itself, with no aura of retrogression or refuge.

"I DO WANT TO TEACH!"

I'm going to be a revolutionary English teacher. At least I hope so. But all this may beat it out of me.

I'm going to be a teacher because I want to be a genuine, practicing intellectual like Mr. Parker!

These were outstanding students who *were* thinking about becoming teachers for a number of reasons. The girl who made the first comment quoted above found her English course "stifling and confining—I'm getting desperate!" She was determined to do a better job when *she* taught, and she hoped somehow to keep her eagerness and idealism alive until she had the chance. Whether this girl's feeling toward the teacher was justified or unfair, or whether her ambition was idealistic or self-dramatizing, the desire to do the job better was a strong motive for her. This type of motive may attract some good students to the teaching profession.

The boy who wanted to be "an intellectual like Mr. Parker" had encountered a teacher whom he described as "a wonderful guy, the kind who uses his brains for humanity, who really makes an adventure out of teaching." Surely the desire "to be like Mr. Parker" is another urge that can draw able people toward a teaching career.

"AIM HIGH—BE A TEACHER!"

On the bulletin board of one of the schools was a large colored poster that showed a huge rocket taking off into space. The caption beside it, in bold letters, read: *AIM HIGH—BE A TEACHER!* A great many of the students I encountered would greet this poster with derisive laughter. Or they might experience a momentary twinge of conscience, as in the case of the boy who said the idea of being a teacher might "take hold of you for a moment when you weren't looking." And for some, it really might carry a sense of aiming high for intellectual challenge and personal adventure.

The story told in the next chapter shows high school students coming to grips with teaching in a way that was new to them. The experience was illuminating for twenty seniors, and may prove to be one of many promising ways our schools can counteract the negative pressures that led one boy to say in his class, "I'd see myself dead before I'd be a teacher!"

CHAPTER 12

TWENTY STUDENTS TRY TEACHING

Good idea

"A new sense of what teaching is all about. . . ." The boy who wrote these words had achieved just that in an experiment he and some friends had carried on in their school. For him, a tremendous push toward teaching as a profession had come as a result of his actual experience of teaching. He was one of twelve boys and eight girls who, as seniors, sought opportunities to teach small groups of younger students in their own school. Some teachers had been sympathetic enough with the idea to work out a schedule for groups to meet regularly, each with one of the seniors as its teacher. Some of the groups developed their own plans—books to be read, writing to be done, research to be pursued. Others followed up special work from the regular courses.

One senior boy led his eighth-grade "class" into a discussion of young people's desire to join, to be part of things. He encouraged these eighth-graders to read Orwell's *1984*, Steinbeck's *Of Mice and Men* and Crane's *The Red Badge of Courage*. One senior girl, with her tenth-graders, explored some aspects of the times of Julius Caesar, beyond the textbook's bounds. One boy had his group study the writings of Erasmus. In another boy's group the focus was on certain mathematical principles and problems. All the pupils who took part in this experiment were volunteers. They met with their senior-teachers regularly during the second semester, usually once and sometimes twice a week, in free periods.

The report written by the students who launched this venture was mimeographed for the school, and the section called "Seniors as Professors" described some interesting discoveries about the process of teaching:

. . . the senior teachers learned more than their pupils. Much of what the student-teachers learned was not immediately pleasant. For many the

experience was one of frustration with little reward, a situation which nobody enjoyed (teacher or student) and which failed to improve noticeably
as the weeks passed. The experiment did, however, lay bare many of the
fallacies in our educational system.

Emerging Problems

Some of the problems which emerged were: the difficulty of teaching
students so "teacher-centered" that when someone too young or "unofficial"
to fit the role of teacher attempted to teach, the students took a recess;
students so "teacher-centered" that they would talk only to the teacher and
never listen or speak to one another; the difficulty of working with students
so mark-conscious that when they discovered that they would not be graded
in this special work, they were noticeably shaken and at a loss for conceiv-
ing any possible reason for being in the classroom. . . .

Problems and Revelations for the New "Teachers"

However, the problems faced by the senior teachers did not all arise from
their pupils. Rather there was one other major source of difficulty—the
seniors themselves. As the tables were turned, the seniors were forced to
grapple with completely new emotions and to enforce a different kind of
discipline upon themselves: the first time nobody did the "terrific" assignment the teacher gave out, or the time nobody seemed interested, or the
time one student talked the entire time while another never spoke or when a
student knew more than the teacher and neither was quite up to admitting
it. There was also the problem of course content. Those who taught what
the faculty teacher assigned had, for the most part, rougher going and less
reward than those who were given the freedom to decide upon their own
content. Another problem was trying to bring forth a point without manipu-
lating or raising questions and without loading them. All of these difficulties
and more arose to surprise and in some cases overwhelm the senior teachers
as several dropped out and others carried on with a new sense of what
teaching was all about.

A NEW VISION OF TEACHING

All the discoveries were not discouraging, however. The report includes these findings as well:

In attempting to evaluate the success and significance of this experiment
we found two things high up on the positive side of the ledger. For one,

the actual experience of teaching gave reality to problems such as teacher-centeredness, marks consciousness, and the effort to discuss rather than merely manipulate under the illusion of discussion. All of these problems we actually *experienced* from the front of the room and they have given solidity to our committee's discussions.

The other respect in which the experiment of "seniors as professors" was unquestionably a success was that it destroyed for all time, in the minds of those who taught, and for their classmates to whom they related their experiences, the conception of teaching as a profession for those persons too nostalgic and weak ever to really leave school and enter into the "real world." The seniors perceived that the real scholarship involved in teaching is extensive research into the *self*, not mere indulgent introspection, but intelligent cultivation of concern. This involves creation of a discipline and the perpetual need to grow toward the point of view and action that teachers worthy of the name must in some part attain: that summit upon which the teacher and student are *together* in their search and in the recognition of the reality of their quest toward truths unseen, unspoken, even hitherto unsought.

The experience of these twenty seniors and their "students" should not be dismissed as one school's eccentricity, or as the work of an unusual cluster of students. The experiment continued the next year with a new senior class. This second year, another twenty students asked to take part. They were allowed to take the initiative in organizing the classes during the first semester, and they had their groups ready for action for the second half-year. Nearly all the first year's seniors worked in history or English. The second year's groups are working in French, biology, general science, and mathematics as well. The vice-principal, who is working with the teaching-seniors this year and who has guided them in their organization and planning, reports:

Nobody claims this work the seniors are doing is going to save any souls among the volunteer pupils. Also, these seniors are not trying to do work that is the faculty's. What is exciting is the way these seniors begin to see some new and, to them, surprising things about *what it means to teach and to learn*. This is the real strength of this business and is why we hope it will continue and develop as it seems to be doing.

Here again is evidence that there are resources available among our high school people which are sometimes ignored or suppressed. The work of these seniors points to one way of opening up a new vision of what teaching and learning can be: not by indoctrination or recruitment, but by challenge and opportunity.

PART FOUR
The Crush for College Admission

CHAPTER 13

YOU SACRIFICE LEARNING FOR MARKS!

School is not a place to get educated in. It's to get you into college.

I heard many comments like this in five of the eight schools I visited. These schools were situated in communities where the students and their parents were anxiety-ridden about the intense competition for admission to "prestige" colleges. In contrast, the students in the other three schools seemed puzzled when I mentioned the idea of tension about college admission.

The students in the schools where the tension was evident seemed to be torn by conflicting objectives. As one boy put it, "Our real aim—to grow intellectually—is blocked by this terrific marks-for-college hassle." In his school, an all-academic public high school with selective admissions, this idea of growing intellectually was expressed so frequently that I could only assume that the students were vitally concerned about it. Yet to them this objective seemed to be at odds with what one girl bitterly called "the neurotic obsession with college admission around here," and with what one boy called "this insane overemphasis on preparation for college."

The pressure starts early. It isn't just a matter of a little stimulating competition in the high school years. One description of the beginnings of the pressure reads like this:

I guess it began around the sixth grade in our community. The principal of the high school came over to our school to talk to us about college. I remember going home that night and asking my family if they thought I'd be able to get into college. That kind of thing pretty well conditions you from the sixth grade on. If you get it bad enough, there is really no room for intellectual expansion. You sacrifice learning for marks.

73

REGENTS TENSIONS

Several New York schools offered conspicuous examples of the effects of pressures on the intellectual life of students. In these schools, students and teachers spoke of increased tensions which they attributed to the Regents examinations system. Some students described the constricting, frustrating routine of "boning up for the Regents." The kind of penetrating study that ambitious students and teachers said they would like to see in their classes seemed out of the question because of the combined effects of the college crush and the examinations.

The notion that "every tenth of a point is crucial in college admissions" would crop up in class after class. And with it would come talk about the Regents examinations' tendencies to dampen student interest and discourage intellectual exploration. One teacher said, "The Regents exams and the College Board subject-matter exams should be designed to give a kid a chance to show how he can handle really challenging questions, but they don't always do this." Another teacher added: "I am all for having ways to maintain standards in schools. The Regents exams usually help us do that, but in some instances they may actually lower our standards of teaching when we feel that we are forced to make a course a memory ordeal to give our students adequate preparation for one of the exams."

MR. WHITE OR MR. GREEN?

Add to the Regents examinations' pressures the stress resulting from other tests and classroom grading in the "college admissions hassle" and you can understand the situation I found in an advanced biology class of seniors. We were talking about kinds of teaching. To summarize what had been said, I offered a quick description of the approaches to teaching which had been pictured in the discussion:

Take first *Mr. White*: he has a strong personality, he presents the material excitingly, and it is expertly, clearly organized. He offers the material to the class *as a group,* has little encounter with any individuals in the class as people. He selects the questions and the grounds for discussion himself. He does a good deal of lively, vigorous lecturing.

Mr. Green is rather quiet, and you sometimes have difficulty seeing what is back of his questions. Most of his work is in organizing questions and activities which get the students into action on their own initiative. The members of the class have a good deal to do with how well an activity or a class period goes. He does not "run" the class, but he sets up plenty of challenge for any member who wants to take it.

I noticed responsive nods as I described each type of teaching, since my descriptions had come from what the students had been saying. After the two descriptions, I asked, "Which of these two kinds of teaching do you prefer?" There was a pause, some looking around, then one boy spoke out: "Which teacher would mark easier?"

In a burst of relief, as if "the real issue" had emerged, these advanced biology students plunged into talk about the fight for marks and scores. As the bell rang, they were beginning to agree on a conclusion which seemed to appall them. Yet they said it was realistic in relation to their own motives. Their conclusion was that their main concern would *have* to be, "Which one would give the highest marks?" because of "the terrific business of getting into college." Kinds of teaching dropped out of sight. The marks issue took over.

These students were impressively bright young men and women. Their acceptance of the marks-for-college drive was not perfunctory, but all-important. They regretted it, and they did not appear to be using it as an excuse for evading broad, explorative study, though this marks issue could be used that way. The teacher reinforced his students' comments after class when he told me:

You know, a lot of times I really think these students would like it best if they were given a perfectly worked-out, mimeographed course, with test questions mimeographed too, with blanks for the answers and a separate answer sheet from which to memorize the answers. And these are my brightest people! They ought to be searching deeply into the subject!

He didn't speak with any special bitterness, and he didn't seem critical of the students. He saw his students trapped in some kind of race, and he hated it.

"WHAT MARK DID YOU GET?"

I often heard a school's whole academic program discussed solely in terms of marks. Among some students who were talking about the emphasis on sports in their school, one said, "It's not just sports that are important. Marks count around here, too." Then the talk shifted to whether sports or marks were stressed more, and by which groups within the school. As these students went on, I saw clearly that they were using "marks" as a label for *the whole academic experience*. They were evidently making a distinction between the *experience* of sports and the *fact* of marks. They were not weighing the *experience* of sports against the *experience* of intellectual activity. Toward the end of the discussion, I pointed this out and one student retorted: "It *has* to be that way because of college." For him, "because of college" was an automatic, all-embracing explanation.

"THE STRIVER"

The terminology used in talking about people's behavior in the college admissions crush varied from one school to another. In one school, students talked about "the striver." Yet it appeared that often a student was divided within himself on the merits of "striving" in courses and in activities. As one boy said, "These 'strivers' join clubs and go out for activities just to get it on their high school record. Of course, I must say I have done this too, but I also join some things which I really care about and have real interest in."

Many college admissions officers have publicly decried the idea of a huge list of activities as a "must" on a college application blank. Yet the "pad-the-activities" aspect of college admission appeared very strong in student thinking. "The problem," one girl said, "is how to 'strive' and, at the same time, maintain your integrity and even get something of an education!" Some "strivers" tried to stay out of advanced courses on the grounds that their marks might look better if they led in the regular classes. Others are "in there pounding to get the teacher to raise a mark from an 89 to a 90, or up from a 94 to a 95." Still others are signing up for every club and activity in the school, even those meeting at the same time on the same afternoon. In one school in a high-powered community, two tenth-grade boys sought me out to tell me about "how the strivers work around here." One said, "Tomorrow at the 12:35 lunch period we'll bring you a real, honest-to-goodness striver and you can see for yourself!"

The next day, at 12:35, the two boys escorted their Striver Exhibit into the psychologist's office, where I had been stationed. "Here he is, a real striver. Talk to him!" one said, and the two boys sat down to listen. The "Exhibit" stood there in puzzled dismay. This was too much for me, and I suggested we all go to lunch.

THE COLLEGE BOARDS

The College Board examinations still create an emotional hurdle, even though they no longer have the curriculum-limiting, restrictive quality of the subject examinations of thirty years ago. The College Board aptitude tests are regarded with special awe. Refusing to accept the aptitude evaluation obtained from the eleventh-grade trial run on these tests, some students (with parental backing) press the schools for cramming sessions for the senior-year aptitude tests, seeking vocabulary-list drills and test-taking tricks. Some amusing incidents result from these attempts to cram. One girl reported: "I heard you could really raise your College Board aptitude scores by outside reading. I told a friend of mine that. She was crazy to get her scores up, but she said, 'Isn't there some workbook or something? I *hate* to read!' "

I asked where her friend was applying for admission, and she gave the names of three of the most highly competitive women's colleges. The irony of her friend's hatred for reading in the light of her choices of colleges seemed to go unnoticed.

A BRAVE EFFORT TO BEAT THE SYSTEM

I met some students who fought this whole pressure as hard as they could. It was a brave fight, with "getting something that amounts to an education" right there in high school as the goal. But for most of these students the experience of one eleventh-grade boy would be very true-to-life:

In the summer session last year, I arranged to take a biology course that I really liked. I was determined that this summer course would be for learning, not for marks. Every now and then the mark would pop into my mind, but I could pretty well get rid of it. I succeeded pretty well during the summer. It was great! I was thinking about what was actually going on in biology. But this fall I can't seem to keep this attitude. I find that I'm constantly computing averages.

CHAPTER 14

"THIS MASS HYSTERIA" AND THE STUDENT

I feel that during the junior high school years most parents want their children to learn and explore and grow. The marks are quite secondary. But during those final three years, parents get desperate about "the right college," and about the things they read about college admissions competition in the papers and magazines. And the whole emphasis on marks and competition suddenly becomes dramatic and loaded with pressure.

This was the mother of two high school students speaking. The school and community tension about college admissions was strung tight at the time of my visit. This mother recognized that parents often play a part in building up this kind of stress. Another mother added, "But you have to remember we're on the receiving end of all this terrifying talk about admissions offices being overwhelmed with applications from valedictorians." The mothers were searching for ways that would help their community to cope with what one called "the mass hysteria that hits the homes around here about the middle of the eleventh grade, or earlier."

One mother said, "I wonder if it is a form of cheating for parents to send their children to tutoring schools to cram for the National Merit Scholarship examinations? A number of parents do this—they say it's a good investment." The others seized on this as an example of the kind of thing that builds tension into panic in their community during the "college-pressure years." They questioned the motivation involved in sending students to private preparatory boarding schools because they felt that such schools usually have special rapport with admissions officers and sometimes use high-powered methods to prepare students for examinations. One of the mothers asked, "Is this fair play any more than sending youngsters to tutoring schools to cram for the National

Merits?" The mothers admitted that many parents don't worry about "fair play" at all. And one added: "This mass hysteria hits especially hard in families that can't afford to send their children to special cram schools or preparatory schools."

These comments came with special urgency:

We have to remember that our children face this hysteria daily.

Doesn't some of the responsibility for all this lie with the colleges? Is it all *our* fault?

And how about the schools—is there anything they can do? This tension really cuts down on intellectual study that amounts to anything. Couldn't teachers——

Is all this business just a fiction? I read last week that hundreds of accredited colleges opened this year without a full enrollment.

Yes, but as far as our children are concerned, it isn't just a matter of an accredited college. It's the feeling that there's only *one* right college!

THE STUDENTS BUILD UP SOME STEAM OF THEIR OWN

It could be that some high school students use this college-admission issue as a kind of emotional kick. Others may use the marks-for-college pressure as a convenient, single motive to avoid facing the more complicated challenges of genuine intellectual exploration. But why is this emotional kick needed at all? And why would a single dramatic motive be more satisfying to these young people than the more tenuous but far more enriching motives that getting an education can involve?

If parents do their part to foster this college admissions anxiety, surely students do theirs. They frequently stressed "that crucial one-tenth of a point" that seemed to blot out so many other possible challenges in a course. They spoke as if they were experts on "what the colleges want"—what activities, what academic averages, what traits of personality, what leadership qualities. The students were far more specific about these "requirements" than most college admissions officers would ever be in public, and perhaps even in private.

THE TEACHERS PITCH IN

Some teachers eagerly capitalize on the college-admission incentive to get their students to achieve step-by-step mastery in the major subject areas. If the students show no signs of intellectual interest in the subject-matter itself, the admissions threat is right there to keep them on their toes. The get-into-college motive seems to be emotionally satisfying to the students as an impetus for going into action academically. Any teacher would surely agree that better reasons could be found, but perhaps none of the others seem so simple and immediate to the student.

In a school where the college admission pressure is pushing the students against the walls, a teacher can ask, "What's your average, Joe?" and Joe will answer instantly, "75," or "B-plus," or "89.43." In the college crush, Joe will have his average on the tip of his tongue, computed from the latest figures. If the teacher wants Joe to put on a little more steam, all he needs to say is: "Better get that average up, Joe! You'll never make college that way!" Notice that no specific college is identified. It often sounds as though "college" were a single, elusive, universal objective—almost a Holy Grail. Concerned teachers and guidance officers struggle hard to counteract this notion. But how can they even begin to convince people that there are *many* kinds of colleges, challenges, subjects for study, and approaches to learning that can come under the heading of "college?"

A roomful of tenth graders were taking a crack at this subject. They knew the problem. They watched their own juniors and seniors—and teachers. These were their "three main ways teachers could *increase* the college admission tension:"

Read the marks aloud and then hand the tests back in the sequence of the marks.

Say, "Why can't you do as well as Joe, who got an'A'?" or "Look at the beautiful work Marian does! Let's try to be a little more like *her* in our attitude toward work."

Tell the students who get low marks on a test: "Well, you're not going to get into college with work like that!"

Then they cited three ways teachers could *play down* the marks-for-college tension in favor of other motives and values:

Hand back the tests and say, "Your mark is your business. Please don't bother to try to find out your neighbor's mark."

Be consistent in marking, so the kids don't feel *in* with you some days and *out* on others.

Don't post the marks on the bulletin board.

Many teachers and guidance officers seemed particularly aware of the college admissions tensions. They saw, too, that their efforts to reassure and give perspective often seemed lonely and futile in the face of national publicity, parental pressure, student panic, and little help from the colleges themselves.

WHO IS REALLY HIT BY THIS PROBLEM?

"A" students and generally successful, above-average students in college-preparatory classes might seem to be those hardest hit by the college admissions panic, but it doesn't always turn out this way. It is true that "A" students may be particularly tense about getting and keeping those A's and gaining admission to the most competitive colleges. These are the colleges to which such students feel, or are led to feel, *they owe it to themselves to apply*. Students ranking just below these top scholars, and less able students, too, may feel the same pressures. Students and teachers alike talked about "kids who are not super-high-powered" being swept into the college rat race. Some parents feel they owe it to their child to "get him into college," and into that so-often undefined "good" college. An average student can struggle with the high school work and fight frustration every day, and then become obsessed with a sense of personal failure if he doesn't make one of the "right" colleges.

The problem also appears to hit their classmates who are not bound for college. In some schools, the "general" student has a hard time, feels himself in a kind of vacuum between the college group and the commercial or vocational groups. General students often envision the college group as people with a clear, immediate, absorbing motive. The vocational and commercial students have specific jobs they are preparing for. So a general student can feel doubtful about the focus of his school experiences and, with this, doubtful about their value.

Commercial students had their version of this story in one of the schools. One boy said, "You have to be either *college prep* or a *girl* around here to have school be any use. The girls in commercial can be secretaries. But what about us? Who wants a male secretary on his lap?"

Vocational students run into some by-products of the tension and fascination of college admissions pressures. They may feel that the school's main concern is with college preparation and college admissions. Some teachers are inept enough to make it clear that they are sorry they have to teach vocational sections. Some vocational students believe the college preparatory group ignores them or discriminates against them in school activities and responsibilities. The comment made by one teacher reveals her view of the relationship of college preparatory students to "the others":

Mary is an awfully able girl, and a lovely one. We have had some trouble guiding her toward a really challenging college. It is the same in her social life. She goes with one of the vocational boys. He's an awfully nice boy, but she doesn't seem to realize that she could do so much *better*.

Thus, anxiety about college admissions can touch *all* parts of a school. The "A" student can respond by driving to get into the most competitive college. The middle student in the college-preparatory program has to compromise his desire for entering the most competitive colleges with more realistic, if unloved, second choices. The student of limited ability, also in the college program, can struggle along and try to handle his frustration and guilt at not being able to make himself fit his image of college-bound achievement. And the general student, the business student, and the vocational student can fail to see and respect their own motives and their own curricula because "the school" seems preoccupied with college admissions as *the* main concern.

PART FIVE
The Need for Responsibility

CHAPTER 15

CONCERN AND ACTION

We have a great student council here!

Student government around here is a farce!

Contradictions such as this invariably arose whenever student responsibility came up for discussion. Most schools now have some form of student government, but the question is, "What does it do?" or "What is its impact?" I attended serious meetings of student councils in the schools. I heard the justifications: "Our student council plans dances, takes care of finances for student activities, discusses school problems—"; and the attacks: "The student government in this school is nothing! It doesn't deal with anything that really matters." I also became aware of the marked contrast between the triviality of some student government activities and the significance of others.

Students were always ready to explain the mechanics of student government: who voted, who was elected to represent whom, what committees were set up. Proponents of student government praised it because it got students involved in respectable thought and action. An eloquent statement for the negative side came from the boy who said: "You know the pathetic thing is *not* that student government activities are so piddling and meaningless. The pathetic thing is that we discuss and vote and carry out these activities *so solemnly*, as if they really *did* amount to something!"

If things are so trivial in the realm of student government, it might be fair to ask whether they should be going on at all. Some students spoke cynically about "responsibility being tested in unimportant areas where it is safe."

In nearly all the schools, the leaders seemed to be the ones who were most enthusiastic. One boy said, "Being elected class president was the most important thing that ever happened to me in school." Notice, though, that he said "being elected"—the *fact* of the vote of

87

confidence. He didn't say anything about the *experience* of serving in office. Another student association president was launching into his job with high hopes for "radical changes." One student council president gave me some remarkably astute suggestions for questions to raise in my interviews at his school.

Where the student council had members who *did* care, who put their efforts into whatever was to be done, at least *these* students were in action. They rose to the challenge of alerting the rest of the school to the idea that something respectably intelligent went on in the student council meetings. I was increasingly on the lookout for activities that students did not pass off as trivial, opportunities for student responsibility which *did* matter. Following are some examples which I encountered in a city school of five thousand students.

CONCERN AND RESPONSIBILITY

I entered the front hall early in the morning and had to push through throngs of students gathered around a huge bulletin board. I saw this written on it when I got close enough to read:

LOOK OVER YOUR CANDIDATES CAREFULLY
FOR THE CITIZENSHIP AWARD
Candidates for Primaries
Vote for Three:
Nelson Rockefeller
Averell Harriman
Danny Kaye
Marian Anderson
Jerry Lewis
Helen Hayes

Beside the poster was a large photograph showing Mrs. Franklin D. Roosevelt on the auditorium stage, accepting her award from the president of the student body the year before. Nearby I saw a huge board with a printed request for foreign-born students to sign under the name of their native country since the school was forming a "little United Nations" within its walls. UN material was displayed on surrounding boards and posters. Later in the morning, I asked about the citizenship award, and a tall, distinguished-looking Negro boy explained: "Each year we vote our award to someone who has rendered some kind of community service that we think is especially fine. Mrs. Roosevelt came last year to get her award and she talked with us!"

This boy took me to the student council meeting to witness the process of choosing the winner of this award. About sixty students were present. One boy rose to speak to the group about "his" candidate, one of the six listed on the poster. The council's faculty adviser whispered to me that each speech was a summary of biographical information that had been gathered and of discussions that had been held in the homerooms. In each homeroom, students had talked about the award, researchers had presented information about the candidates, and then nominating votes had been taken. This way, the whole school was in on the process of thinking and studying about the candidates.

To make sure that all students were kept informed about the student council activities in this school, the delegates were required to report on the council meetings to their homeroom classmates. Each delegate would sign a mimeographed form and return it to the council to show that he had completed his report. Thus the council tried to keep in touch with all the homerooms—with five thousand students. Here was one way of getting unity from a large student body of tremendous diversity.

Marian Anderson, Danny Kaye, and Nelson Rockefeller were selected in the preliminary balloting. Rockefeller was probably the most famous man in their city. Both Marian Anderson and Danny Kaye were much on the minds of the students because of their recent intensive attempts to promote international good will. The school's keen interest in UN affairs seemed closely related to the admiration and respect felt for these two people.

DANNY KAYE WINS!

Danny Kaye's "victory" was greeted as big news in the halls as the word began to spread. Evidently his continued service to the United Nations had captured the imagination and appreciation of these students. The memorable television program that showed his UN work with children around the world had been seen at least two years ago. He had appeared in only a few films during the past several years. If the students in this school wanted to reward an entertainer, they could have chosen many others more sensationally popular with teen-age society than Danny Kaye.

THE COMMISSIONS OF THE CABINET

I came across the "cabinet's commissions" meeting at this same school, where heads of a number of commissions were reporting. A boy of Puerto Rican background reported zestfully for the "Seven Arts Commission," discussing plans for one-act plays. He made a plea for going ahead with these in spite of the number of dropouts of prospective actors following the appearance of the first report cards. Reports followed from the "Save the Children Federation," the "Parents Association Commission," and the "Publicity Commission." Other student government "commissions" functioning were:

Alumni Association	Publicity
Budget	Sales
Clubs	Service Society
Election	Student Government Membership
The Citizenship Award	Social Affairs
Judicial Affairs	Isabella Home (a neighborhood home for the aged)

These commissions seemed interesting and important to the students. They involved action, much of it outside the school, and the administration seemed to give them genuine prestige. They were regarded with esteem by the students and teachers.

STUDENTS AND THE CURRICULUM

It is easy to assume that the curriculum is "not the students' business." Yet, if the students are allowed no voice in the curriculum, other than to give the right anwers in class, some good opportunities to stimulate their intellectual interest and curiosity are missed.

I stumbled upon an example of hearty student interest in the curriculum when I attended a meeting of the Forum Club in this same school. The chairman was the president of the senior class. He was a tall, intelligent boy and was holding the attention of the ten students in the group. The student president of the United Nations Club was one of them. The subject was the history curriculum. These students showed such keen perception about what the field of history can offer that I wondered if they were advanced history students with a special interest and background in the subject. But I was enlightened by this significant comment from one of the girls: "I'm a general student and I'm not worried about getting into college, but the things you're talking about mean a lot to me. I could really get interested in exploring and thinking about them."

The chairman drew on this girl's thinking a good deal for the discussion, especially when things got, as he said, "too balled up in what is supposed to be needed for college."

A faculty adviser at this meeting sat and read a magazine, looking up now and then to add a thoughtful comment, showing her alertness and interest, but displaying no tendency to control or dominate the session. There was no question about this being a *student* affair.

It would be interesting to see where these students go with their thinking on the history curriculum. Will it result in a set of questions, recommendations, further meetings, planning with teachers, or perhaps designing experimental projects? One can be sure of this: the students were eager and astute in their discussion of what history had to offer, and what kinds of exploration they would like to be doing in this subject area.

"THE UN IS A BIG THING AROUND HERE . . ."

This school showed keen interest in the United Nations. The sources of this interest are well worth noting. An alert social studies department seemed eager to keep the students aware of UN ideals and activities. The cooperative efforts of the United Nations Club and the International Relations Club, working with art and publicity committees, also generated enthusiasm. In addition the school draws from a wide variety of neighborhoods and families, with the result that its students represent diverse racial, national, and economic backgrounds.

I discovered another major clue. That was when I was attending a

meeting of about ten teachers, each from a different department in
the school, who were forming a faculty committee on the United
Nations. It was fascinating to see these teachers explore, argue, and
plan together. Their different points of view sprang from their backgrounds in French, modern dance, speech, and mathematics, as well
as from their varied personal, religious, and political tenets. They
wanted to see what they could do toward widening student interest
in the United Nations' work and improving understanding of international issues. A boy who was the head of the student United Nations
Club attended the meeting and he spoke eloquently. He and a classmate had conducted public inter-school discussions of the UN the
week before. Their discussions had been covered in the city newspapers and had received extensive publicity within the schools concerned.

Focus on the UN did not stop at study and observation. Each of
more than fifty homerooms in the school was supporting a child somewhere in the world, through student contributions to special agencies.

The "little United Nations" in the school was growing fast and it
already had representatives of thirty-two nationalities. In a conversation with me, the student-president of the United Nations Club expressed this sobering thought: "We want to make very sure we don't
expect the 'little UN' delegates to represent the position of the government of the country they were born in. Their families may have left
because they didn't go for that position!"

In a social studies class for "slow learners," a boy asked permission
to speak for a moment at the beginning of the period. He stood up at
his desk and gave a sincere and dignified plea for people to bring in
clothing and blankets for an American Indian tribe about which he
had given a report. "We are so tied up with people in other countries
that we should be careful not to forget people who are in trouble here
—people our country helped to make poor." I met this boy later and
asked him how he happened to become interested in this particular
tribe. He said: "Well, the school's full of projects about different kinds
of people and different countries. I read a story once about this bunch
of Indians, and I went and asked my minister if there was anything
I could do to help them."

From then on the minister and the boy appealed to a number of young people in the community and sparked a lot of interest and activity in helping the tribe. It is hard to tell whether the school, the boy, or the responsive minister deserves principal credit for this enterprise, but I suspect the school's climate of concerns and responsibilities had a great deal to do with it.

CHAPTER 16

SEVEN SENIORS STUDY THEIR SCHOOL

I like to see connections, the whole sweep of the past. It gives you a feeling of belonging.

This boy was being interviewed by a classmate, one of seven seniors who had launched a remarkably challenging and constructive study of their own school. Their enterprise was, interestingly enough, an off-shoot of the project that I was conducting.

I had taken an unusually perceptive senior boy with me to visit one of the schools, with the intention of turning him loose in the school to explore and question on his own during my stay. I hardly saw this boy during my visit to the school, but the conversations he had in the locker room and parking lot, in classrooms and the cafeteria, brought rich material to this report. During his time as a visitor he became curious about his own school and what might happen if some of this kind of questioning and self-examining were to take place there. He returned home, sought the support of a half-dozen congenial class-mates, and in a few days launched a project which became a significant adventure.

These seven seniors wanted to work both with students and teachers to throw some light on the *what's* and *why's* in the life of their school. They were hard at work on this enterprise throughout the last five months of their senior year. Just how they found the time for the interviews, the meetings with each other, the planning, the writing, and the mimeographing of their report for release on Commencement Day, I cannot guess. All of them were carrying heavy loads of academic work, but somehow they managed. Their report was a remarkable document. Out of a whole series of frank talks with teachers, administrators, classmates, and some younger students came a vision of achievements, problems, and possibilities in one school which has al-

94

ready evoked considerable interest beyond those walls. My guess is that the experience was worth more to the seven seniors and to the teachers and students who worked with them than any printed report can be to others. Yet the report speaks out vigorously and is worth a close look.

THE REPORT

The students' report begins by telling about the teaching adventures of twenty seniors.* Then it explores such problems as: How do you get the word around a school about courses and what they are all about? Another part presents some ideas about the "haves" and the "have-nots" in the school, the people who seem to have all the opportunities as council-members, presidents, chairmen, delegates—the busy ones—and the people who just sit and wish they could have some responsibility but "never get asked."

"THE OMNIPOTENT SCHEDULE"

A section on scheduling raises questions about the length of class periods, and recognizes a sadly obvious fact in a statement from one of the seniors interviewed: "If you are enjoying a class, forty minutes is ridiculously short, but if it's a dull class, it's years too long!"

The seniors look at some experiments in the school about period length and go on to some disturbing questions about ". . . the strange compulsion in so many schools to have each course meet daily and for forty minutes, regardless of how much time is really needed and in what kind of chunks."

"THE ILLUSION OF DISCUSSION"

This chapter title leads to a stiff criticism of students and teachers. The writers say:

. . . discussion is an illusion when the teacher holds in his mind a preconceived notion of *the* conclusion to be reached and *the* method to be used to reach the conclusion.

. . . the teacher proceeds to stimulate guessing by handing out various

* Chapter 10.

hints as to what he wants. The result is that an exchange of ideas in search of new questions or conclusions does not take place. Rather, the student, who has become aware that the teacher has a set answer he hopes to evoke, ceases to think. He merely tries to read the mind of the teacher. Thus, with many anxious hands and voices, the illusion of discussion has been created.

The students also warn of this danger:

. . . when the teacher sets his mind up as the interpreter and judge of all that is said by the student, the class can move only as fast and as far as the teacher's mind. There cannot be discussion among students because each statement must first *pass the test of the teacher's mind* before it becomes valid or even worthy of discussion. Students cease to talk to one another but talk only to (and often for) the teacher.

The report of the teaching seniors' experiences in working on the other side of the desk revealed they had become startlingly aware of the difficulties of teacher's task. "Discussion is all the rage," one of the seniors said, "but we wonder if by the eighth or ninth grade a lot of students have any concept of discussion." They explain:

. . . when asked to speak to one another and not only to the teacher, some students are embarrassed and amazed. Respect for contemporary opinion is lost as they cease to even listen to one another. The teacher figure is king; the students are vessels to be filled with all the perceptions and limitations of the teacher's vision.

Their hope is this:

The remedy for this situation is not simple. We feel, however, that teachers should allow students to teach each other and themselves. When teachers feel something is so factual as to defy variations or a new approach they would save time if they would lecture. Then upon less concrete matters and on *real* questions they should allow actual discussion among the students to occur. The illusion of discussion is the illusion of education and the illusion of individual importance. *Real* discussions will evolve *real* respect for subject matter and for one's classmates.

"THE SEARCH FOR UNITY"

In the next section, the students make a plea for "unity," which they define this way:

. . . a student's sense of a significant relationship either between a course one year and another in the same department the next year, or between two different courses in the same year, or between himself and any given course, or between the courses he takes and the world around him.

Teachers' and students' thoughtful opinions on ways of attaining some of these kinds of "unity" are quoted. The students stress the need to remember that courses should be designed for *human beings*:

Reverence for subject matter means belittling what any student "feels" or "thinks" about the material. Ironically, this "feeling" or "thinking" is the stuff of learning. It is the core of any significant education. The school can allow each student to come to terms with the subject matter only by giving him freedom and by respecting his use of that freedom.

An appeal for encouraging the expansion of this freedom ends the section:

The committee realizes that many people fear freedom for students. . . . People rise to heights and fall to depths almost in direct proportion to what is expected of them. It is only in an atmosphere of freedom, an atmosphere in which students can respond to their own impulses to explore, that education becomes meaningful. There are dangers, but they are part of the challenge, a challenge that must be met if students like the one quoted below are to have their wish:
"I like to see connections, the whole sweep of the past. It gives you a feeling of belonging."

"THE REALITY OF IDEALISM"

The seniors use this title for a description of experiments in their school which seem exciting and important to them. In these experiments, their school had set aside a whole day exclusively for music and another day for religion. The programs for both special days involved students from other schools as well as this one. Both were carefully planned by students, with interested and sympathetic help from key teachers. Both programs seemed to achieve something extraordinary in morale. The report states:

This was education. This was a group of human beings searching and questioning. Because the existence of the conference assumed that the students were responsible and mature, they were. As one senior boy said, voicing his amazement at his classmates' interest and concern:

"Hey, we have been tricked. I just found out that today is Saturday!"

Imagine, learning something on a Saturday!

The two days stand as two concrete examples of the "reality of idealism." The educational value of these two projects should raise many questions about the numerous days that nobody ever mentions or remembers.

CHAPTER 17

LEADERS OR JUST ELECTION WINNERS?

. . . What we do need is a more mature recognition of ourselves as individuals. . . .

This sounds odd in a campaign speech for a top position of leadership in a school. Yet a campaigning senior said it in an extraordinary speech he made a few days before his election as president of the student body. I talked with him after I had heard that he had been elected. He was anxious, he told me, ". . . to hit this idea of the individual student's part in creating this school. I thought it would really make more sense to come out and say this was the whole point, and not bother with the usual rigmarole of a platform and all that."

This fragment of his speech may exhibit something of what this boy was trying to get across to his schoolmates modestly and sincerely:

. . . All of us have experienced various degrees of nausea and feelings of identification when a candidate stands up in a meeting in late May and mumbles something about himself and the school and sits down again. This mumble stems from the semiconscious revelation that all along nobody had anything up his sleeve—nobody was making any money out of the students at this school, and the bit about a student-teacher rift was mostly rebellious bosh. In fact, we and our teachers are involved in a process which goes beyond, or rather through, math, French, English—into the essence of our being—as emerging individuals. Yet all we get is a mumble in May of the senior year. I should like to see the mumble become conscious and articulate—and not in May of the senior year but in the sophomore year or earlier.

While I was following his rather surprising words, I was torn between watching him and observing the students around me as they listened. He moved to the subject of school dances. He said, "Now there is the question of school dances," and many people, particularly some girls sitting across the aisle from me, seemed to perk up. Some moved ahead in their seats. "Here we go," one girl near me muttered. The candidate went on:

School dances have long been an area of conflict, and I think that within this conflict can also be seen the lack of recognition of what and where we are and the infinite possibilities for growth in our position. I am not in favor of Big Dances, but I should like very much to have our small dances successful. For some reason, when we dress up, turn down the lights, and turn on the music, everything we have been as a group, gathered together for the mutual exchange of ideas and the individual construction of values, is lost. We denounce materialism all week long, but those with ties that don't match, or with inappropriate dresses, tend to be aware of these factors by the end of a dance.

Some students looked uncomfortable at this. Some looked pleased. Suddenly there was concentrated attention as the boy said this, continuing about dances:

As girls whom we know, respect, and enjoy during the week become suddenly too tall, or too fat, or socially unacceptable, they are pushed off to cringe in the corners. The troops hike outside for a smoke—and people demonstrate their affection for one another as if it were a naughty but joyous repose from the moral eyes of the school. Has not the attraction of male and female been going on long enough (after all we are products of it)——

The auditorium broke into a riot of laughter. The speaker waited a moment. The students quieted down. They didn't want to miss anything. The boy resumed quietly:

Hasn't this attraction been going on long enough so that we can rise above the new destructive forces of low lights and music? Must we mock ourselves and all we say during the week about acceptance and values? We do not need bigger bands and lower lights—but what we do need is a more mature recognition of ourselves as human beings.

"How about this?" a boy just ahead of me said to someone behind him. "Yes, how about it?" a girl muttered, overhearing.

The candidate moved on to a plea for the best insight, the best values that the people in the school could bring into action. He spoke of the interest and concern felt in the school for social problems such as racial prejudice and rejection of minority groups, and the resulting seminars, work camps, petitions, conferences, community surveys:

> Yet, the council which is concerned with the social problems in our own *school* seems rather ineffective. Rejection of minority groups concerns us, yet the rejection of an individual whom one or a class knows personally is far more destructive. For this reason, I am all for the amendment we just passed pertaining to the Advisory Council. I am convinced that with a council working at the class level we can recognize and cope with the some-times irreparable damage we wreak—often in a casual manner—upon our contemporaries. . . .

He kept his audience intent on his words, even during its bursts of surprised laughter at some hilarious thrusts about school mores. He concentrated on the idea of the single individual's contribution and ended with a stress on the need for ". . . freedom to decide, to govern, as individuals, the direction and intensity of our experience together."

I am not sure how much this speech contributed to the boy's election victory, but I do know that the thoughtfulness of his presentation kept his audience enthralled. His ideas seemed to be refreshing and "catching" in that room. Yet they seemed to blend with the general climate of the school. Or better, they seemed to delineate the audience's conception of *what their school community should be like.* Crucial to this vision was the idea of the individual working sometimes *with* others, sometimes *for* others, but always responsible for his own developing values and the welfare of his school.

ENTHUSIASM VS. FACELESSNESS

Leadership seems to be an issue in some schools, quiescent in others, a mocking game in others. I talked with a college preparatory group in one comprehensive high school that had an impressive and effective student president. In trying to point to things that "really mattered" in their high school careers, a number of students spoke of "our leadership." A reflective boy, sitting three seats away from the student president, put it this way:

I think a lot of what's important in our experience here is the kind of leadership we have. We've done really well in this, I think. I mean somehow we have gotten people into top spots who have a lot of enthusiasm, who care a lot. This pays off in the kind of feeling you get in a class.

A girl who had transferred to this school in the eleventh grade spoke up:

I used to be in a school where the idea seemed to be to find the most faceless character in the school and make him a council member, chairman, or president. Things were very competitive there, and there was a lot of jealousy. I guess there had to be someone to elect to things whom nobody could feel jealous of!

WAITING FOR "BARRY"

In an eleventh grade, in another school, the students were talking about their leaders, or lack of them. The name Barry kept cropping up as the students debated about "what's the matter with our class?" Apparently Barry had moved away from the community at the end of tenth grade. One boy said, "That guy was the only one who could handle this class. We haven't got anybody now."

Another added, "You ought to meet that guy. You'd see what we mean." A girl spoke with vehemence and acute nostalgia: "Things seemed to fall apart when he left. I mean there was no one who could make all the different crowds in the class come together."

The class seemed lost, leaderless. There was "no one like Barry."

THE TRIBE'S STRONGEST WARRIOR

"It's one huge popularity contest, and the trickiest trickster wins. I should know, because I won. But I don't like it, and I'm going to do what I can about it."

This was a newly elected student president. He was full of what he called "revolutionary ideas to move things along around here." He seemed serious and ambitious, though doubtful about "what you could do with the kids in this school." He described the campaign that had got him elected and showed me an English paper he had written about it. Even allowing for a large helping of calculated cynicism and "composition license," I found the picture he created both amusing and sad. He delineated the necessary emotional appeals of the student candidate in the rallies: "The tribe's 'strongest-warrior' approach . . . the slightly limping, modest football hero . . . the busy committee organizer . . . the appeal for yaks . . . the barrage of posters . . . the word-of-mouth appeals . . ." He felt he had grasped the situation and had used it. But he did want to change it.

A CLASS IN LEADERSHIP

"How would you like to visit a leadership class?"

The adviser for student activities in a large city school was leading me along the hall and into a little lounge. I went in, and sat down to watch. The meeting was nearly over. About twenty students were deep in a thoughtful discussion about "courtesy and decent morale in the school."

The idea seemed to be that they felt a school of this size was in danger of becoming mechanized and impersonal unless special attention were given to people's behavior toward each other during the rush of the typical school day. They quickly made some plan about approaching the editors of the school paper as the period bell rang.

For a few minutes after they left I listened to what the faculty adviser had to say about this leadership class: "We don't make a big publicity thing out of this. Each year I try to get about twenty-three sophomores and juniors for this class. The homeroom teachers know what we are after and I take recommendations from them or spot some people myself."

I asked him what he really was looking for. He explained:

"We try to get people who seem to have some special potential for leadership. I try, too, for pretty good balance in the racial and national backgrounds we have here in school. Sometimes these students will bring in others who are interested or curious."

I wondered if a stigma might not fall on faculty-planned student meetings for discussing leadership. He jumped to this subject:

"Not so far as I can see. One reason is that there are five thousand students here. A great many of these people go ahead into elected or volunteer spots in the school. Some don't, of course. But we want to try to support these people who have certain values and let them recognize the possibilities in leadership in a school like this."

It seemed to me that there was no reason to press the point about faculty domination, especially since I had not yet heard (and never did hear) anything about it from the students in that school.

This leadership group was one of many activities under this one man. His charges included the student council and the commissions of the student cabinet, described earlier in Chapter 13. He explained:

What we want is to have some potential leaders become a little more sensitive to some of the needs and opportunities around here for student action. I see these people in a number of spots around school, but the discussions in here once a week give us a chance to get some perspective on the school and look at some possibilities. And there really seems to be some carry-over!

It seems well worth noting that here was a large school whose faculty *cared* about developing student responsibility enough to establish a method for promoting it.

PART SIX

Divisive Forces in the School and Community

CHAPTER 18

PREJUDICE

We ought to go into this business about teen-agers not having any concern. People really care around here, care about a lot of things. . . .

I witnessed this concern and caring, particularly in situations that involved divisions among individuals or groups. These divisions sometimes had their origins in the community, sometimes in the school. Divisions based on social prejudice, whatever the origin, seemed to arouse the students the most.

When the boy quoted above began to talk about social prejudice, he —I'll call him Joe—and his friends made some revelations that startled me. Joe sat at the end of a long table, balancing the back of his chair against the wall. There were six of us around the table. Two of the boys had their feet up. It was late in the afternoon, and we were ready to relax. I had been impressed previously by the depth of thinking of these five seniors during several encounters with them in the past two days of my visit. They had called to me to come in as they saw me pass the door. Joe explained:

We have this discussion group every Tuesday night, about twelve of us, and we really go to town. We made a deal that there'd be no adults because we wanted to be absolutely on our own with nobody trying to take it over. It's really great. We fall over each other, get noisy, and yell at each other, but it's really exciting and means a whole lot more to us than any of the homework.

BART: Tomorrow night we talk about Thoreau's essay on civil disobedience. You know it?

ELLEN: Can you come tomorrow night? You really ought to see this crowd in action! [I said I would still be in town and would surely come.]

JOE: Maybe it won't be any good. But it might be. Depends if everybody does the reading. It's pretty miserable if they don't—unless

107

we just hit some bull topic. It doesn't take much to get us into some kind of hot discussion.

TOM: The best session we've had was the one on the Grand Inquisitor scene. This was really good, especially since Joe and Cindy are Catholics. That really did it.

The mention of Catholics shifted the subject suddenly and dramatically to social prejudice. The special prejudice against Jews in their community obviously angered these young people. They leaped from the Grand Inquisitor to the restrictions of the local country club.

TOM: It's pretty rough there. Dave and I tried an experiment. I took him as my guest to one of the teen-age dances at the club, and they didn't let him in. We wondered what would happen and we found out.

ELLEN: This discussion group business really went all out on this prejudice thing last year. Joe and I had gone to some meeting of the National Conference of Christians and Jews. It didn't seem to get anybody anywhere and we wondered if there wasn't something more to do than go to meetings. We thought maybe we could at least make some noise about it.

JOE: We have our own way of kidding about prejudice here in the school. We sometimes get into mock fights and start calling each other wild names like "kike" and "filthy Catholic" and "mick" and what not. The only trouble is, sometimes these are overheard and they really shock people.

BART: Yeah, and a lot of times when this is overheard, some of the people join in in earnest. How about the time Mary overheard Joe and Bob going at it—she came in just as Bob was calling Joe a filthy Catholic. Mary, who is also a Catholic, just walked away. She should have told Joe his remarks were terrible, because she thought he was serious. When people come along and get into the thing seriously, we really have to shift gears in a hurry.

TOM: Once we got a towel from the country club, and hung it up in our locker room just as you walk into it, then we tagged a little sign onto it underneath, "No Jews Allowed." We thought it would be interesting to see what would happen. A lot of people looked and there were a lot of reactions in the first few seconds. Then some kid whose family belongs to the club got really mad and said,

"What the hell is this?" Then he tore the thing down and ripped
up the sign.

They speculated on whether the boy was embarrassed or outraged. Bart
and Dave were Jews, Ellen and Tom were Protestants, and Joe was a
Catholic.

They started to sketch a map of the community on the table. Tom
and Bart were using pads and pencils to set up the town plan: "Here's
how the town works. There are four regions here. Two are just ghettos
—really bad—real ghettos."

It appeared that Bart, Tom, and Dave lived in the "mixed," or desir-
able, areas. Bart continued: "Then one region is all Christian, including a lot of Catholics. And the fourth region is a mixture. There's very
little social mingling."

Tom remarked: "My father's in the club and tries to fight it, but he
says it's hopeless."

I asked: "You mean you think there's nothing you people can do
about this even when you get more influence in the community?"

TOM: Well, you take our parents; they cared about this kind of thing
      and maybe had some pretty good ideas about reforming it, and yet
      they grew up and got established in things and somehow or other
      it didn't happen. Now they sort of sit back and don't push very
      much for any change.
ELLEN: Well, maybe it is like going two steps forward and one step back.
      We might be able to do something.

They seemed to be inclined to give the job up as hopeless. Yet, when
questioned, they did speak up with some optimism. Perhaps they wanted
to believe they really *could* have some impact on the problem. They
were guarded, cautious about the prospects for progress.

Bart answered Ellen:

Yes, there will be some advancement. You have to remember that hardly
anybody who's here in the school was born here. People keep moving here
from all over the country. My folks are from Ohio. Your father's from Cali-
fornia. A lot of people move here for the school. The school really *is* this
community. It's what people hear about. People know that this school is

better than those in other towns in this region. People who want to retire or want to leave see to it that they stay until the kids go through this school. Once they are ready to retire, it's too expensive to stay on here. This school was started only around twenty-five years ago, so maybe we will be able to do *something*.

I had run into the word "prejudice" in earlier discussions in this school. But it had never been defined until this afternoon. Once the issue was out, and other students knew I had heard about it, it became a major focus for later discussion, although I never raised it myself.

The students were torn between eagerness to break down prejudice—to do better than the previous generation—and discouragement at the apparent failure or the apathy they sensed in their parents.

And the school? Some of the history teachers were working on the problem in classes dealing with religions. Their hope was to help break down this kind of prejudice. But, as one student pointed out:

When groups divide up because of religion, it isn't really *religion*—I mean the doctrine or beliefs or anything. It's a *type* of heritage. If homes are similar, if the background and the heritage are the same, then the kids are similar. And they become suspicious of what is *not* similar.

Bob added:

You know, we started a car pool of people who enjoyed going to school together and once it was all formed it turned out that we were all Christians.

Bart summed it up:

Yeah, that's it. You can't say it's a matter of religion. Certainly the church activities and doctrine don't affect peoples' lives around here. Maybe you can't explain heritage, either. It's just something that gets into the kids of any one group, so they seem to be like each other.

I wonder now, as I write this, whether Joe, Bart, Dave, Ellen, and the others will fall back into "you just can't do anything about it" as the years go by. Can a school do anything to help them go on being angry?

CHAPTER 19

"YOU'RE NOTHING IF YOU'RE NOT COLLEGE PREP!"

We don't ever get to meet anybody new. There's just each other!

This statement came from a boy in a classroom full of vocational juniors. He went on to say, "The college prep kids here get all the elected offices. They get the girls, even. And *we* never see them!"

"Yeah," another put in, "a girl takes a look at us in our dungarees on our way to the shop and says, 'Ugh—shop boys!' "

"We don't even *hear* about anything that goes on around here. If a play is being given, the first we hear about it is when we see a sign posted. We usually don't even get to see it."

I asked if any of them would be interested in trying out for one of the school plays.

"Oh no, the college prep kids have that tied up. We wouldn't try out."

I insisted: "But what if you did? Has anybody tried?" These comments followed:

It's not for us; that's the way it is.

And with elected jobs, all we get to do is vote.

You know, you read about college kids doing those crazy things in the dorms. Well, our college prep kids do a lot of that stuff around here. They get away with it. But we get watched pretty close. The girls think it's real cute when the college boys horse around. With us, it's no go.

I wish we could have some class or something here with the girls. But I guess we couldn't. There's no such thing as shop girls.

But why should we be the only people in the school who don't ever have any class or activity with girls?

Asked about things that could change this situation, one boy spoke up for the school's latest effort:

111

The school has helped in one way. They put through this new rule on dress. No dungarees and old shirts in school. They figure if you're dressed up you work and think better.

[This brought a torrent of agreement.]

It's a pain-in-the-neck having to change your clothes at the start and finish of the shop periods, and we get late to the other classes. But still it makes things better.

What's really better is that *now* we get to look like the college prep kids!

Here in the comprehensive high school of an industrial community, I spent two full days with the vocational sections. I was continually impressed by the articulateness of these boys and by the thoughtfulness they showed in examining the insularity they saw in their school. The vocational classes were sectioned according to tested ability with words and numbers. The "slowest" students went at their discussion with as much intensity and concern as the brightest. They showed unusual interest in this study and were very courteous as they listened to each other and to my questions. They seemed to have experiences to report that touched reality more than did those of the college-bound students "upstairs," who were supposedly more fluent with words. Much that these vocational students had to say was negative, yet I felt that their insights could be a real advantage to the school.

These boys were almost obsessed with a feeling of social isolation from the rest of the school. In the brightest of the vocational groups, this subject did not emerge immediately, perhaps because those boys had some confidence in their own ability and worth and were doing particularly well in their work. In that group one major theme never appeared: "I would still be in college prep if it hadn't been for . . ." This was an opening phrase I often heard in the other vocational sections. For one boy, the death of his father lowered his morale so much that he "had to drop out of college prep." For another, it was failure in a course where he had had trouble with the teacher. For another, it was "the school that stuck me in here."

Many of the students seemed convinced that even though the vocational students in the school were so numerous, they were somehow less worthy; they had missed the chance to be something better. One boy summed up the feeling for the rest:

"Around here you're *nothing* if you're not college prep."

I tried to pursue this theme during the rest of my encounters with teachers and college preparatory students in the school. The students in college prep sections seemed vague about the existence of any split between themselves and vocational people. They spoke in stereotypes about vocational students: "kids that are forced to come to school by law," "people that don't really want to learn anything," "hoods." Or else they would say that they weren't aware of any special problem, that "the shop people seem to get around the school and do things like the rest." A few said the vocational group didn't seem to have much "class spirit" and that "you can't force them to do things with the class if they don't want to."

My own encounter with these vocational students had given me such a different picture of the people involved that I began to think that only the *complete* separation of the two groups in the school could account for the college prep students' stereotypes of the vocational boys.

Certain teachers and administrators seemed to recognize the problem caused by this segregation. As one said, "We have a comprehensive high school here, in theory. Actually, we have three separate schools: college prep, general, and vocational. And we can't kid ourselves about what this means in unity—or lack of it."

I asked a number of adults in the school about opportunities provided for the three groups to get together. A basic difficulty seemed to be that of trying to organize the long hours in the various shops to fit the schedule of academic classes meeting for a single period daily. If a boy was in shop for six weeks, full time, it was impossible to put him into a major course, or even a minor course or activity, that had been meeting daily during those six weeks. Thus, the vocational students had separate English classes, for example, and their own schedule operating according to its own system. Even the few chances the different groups had to get together seemed to promote the divisiveness. One vocational boy said, "We all get together in a gym class. But somehow or other it ends up with the college prep kids playing ball in one end of the gym and us doing pushups in the other." One teacher's answer to this was:

The organization of the school makes this almost inevitable. There are three thousand students here. It's asking a lot to expect us to give each of the three groups a program that amounts to something and still have a schedule that allows for mixing the groups together. I just don't see how you'd organize it.

IN A DIFFERENT SETTING

I found some of these same problems in a rural junior-senior high school that had about five hundred students. As in the other school, these students were divided in their educational aims, but here I discovered some interesting situations where social barriers were dissolved.

About thirty-five of the eighty-five seniors were planning to go on to four-year colleges. Another nine or ten were headed for some other kind of higher education. The others—almost half the class—would end their academic life on high school graduation day.

Instead of having separate college preparatory, general, and vocational divisions in this school, the students in each grade are sectioned according to their abilities. Most of the courses have three sections. The strongest college prep students are the mainstays of Section One. A middle group, with some college-bound students, makes up Section Two. Either less able or vocational students (or both) make up Section Three.

Since the vocational students do not automatically end up in "slow section," the "vocational" label has not become a hallmark for dumbness for the students in this school. Vocational students appear in all sections and therefore do not readily conform to stereotypes.

Still, the shining image of the college prep students as "the ones that have it made around here" appeared occasionally in this school.

We always get a college prep class president. And in a meeting when he sees a college prep hand up and one of our hands up, he calls on the college prep hand.

They can make you look pretty stupid in a class meeting if they want to.

Here the students seemed to be conscious of social status in the community as a divisive force. "People in those higher brackets," as one boy called them, "create barriers." Different interests or concerns helped make barriers, too. One vocational senior offered this experience, with some joviality:

Last year I tried out this break-the-barriers deal. I went and sat down at the lunch table with these six higher-bracket girls. They looked right through me and went on talking. They were bubbling on about the problems of the starving Burmese, and when I just asked them to pass the salt they looked at me as if I was the most pitiful clunk that ever was. I had the feeling I was sitting there and yet I wasn't. They just don't *want* to mix.

His classmates took this thoughtfully. Some claimed it wasn't a fair test, but a number of others agreed that this was "pretty much the way it is."

The seniors had just had their election, and the conversation moved to this topic. A college prep student had won by a narrow margin over a boy who had most of his classes in the slow, "number three" section. The class discussed this openly. A ballot-counter said: "Maybe I shouldn't say this, but the election this morning was mighty close. Joe almost won. I was really worried. I didn't think Joe could handle it."

The class listened with interest. Others agreed that Joe would have had a hard time as class president.

"He wouldn't know how to handle the thing."

"He hasn't had the experience."

One girl burst in hotly:

"That's just the point. How are the kids like Joe *ever* to get experience if the jobs always go to the college prep kids?"

Most of the class seemed to side with the ballot-counter who had been worried that "Joe couldn't handle it."

A teacher reminded me later that if the non-college-bound students really wanted to swing an election to one of their own people they could do it easily by solid-front voting. "But they never do this. They really seem to look over the people and choose the one they have most confidence in."

DISSOLVING THE BARRIERS

Every time I asked what experiences in this school tended to weaken barriers and break down social casts, some boy would speak up for athletics. In many schools athletics contribute to *making* the divisions.

But here, in repeated and often moving testimony, boys (but not girls) spoke of athletics as the number one destroyer of barriers:

In athletics it doesn't matter whether a guy is smart or stupid, or whether he comes from a rich home or the lumber camps. The thing that matters is how he plays.

If you're on a team you can go *anywhere*—you're automatically invited. You belong.

In athletics you really get to know people. You're in there—you're one of the gang.

When there's a party for the team, everybody gets invited—whether you sit on the bench or are the hero.

I asked: "In what you said, 'everybody' includes all those who go out for the sport, doesn't it? That's different from 'everybody in a class,' isn't it?"

The boy and his classmates saw the point, but they quickly stressed that the student body was not divided into athletes and non-athletes. "Team members ask their girls and the girls ask their boy friends— everybody goes to the team parties," one student explained.

The boys persistently emphasized that athletics obliterated social and IQ barriers. One boy spoke of his experience in athletics: "You can be on your own in athletics. You're not stuck in a fixed pattern."

In the discussion that ensued, some students clearly interpreted his statement as a comment on rigid and impersonal course work. But most seemed to interpret it as meaning that athletic events in this school enabled students to break out of divisions based on social background, college plans, or academic ability.

CHAPTER 20

"WE'RE THE ADVANCED SECTION!"

I think that just being in this section with these people is one of the most valuable things that has happened to me in school. There are some problems that go with it, though . . .

This girl's comment ran like a recurring theme through the conversations in schools having advanced sections for their brightest students. Enthusiasm and appreciation were proclaimed for "being with these people," but not without some reservations. Sometimes the reservations took over the discussion and sometimes the enthusiasm obliterated the doubts. But it is clear that grouping students by academic ability has more than academic results.

Just how schools arrange these sections varies a good deal. Some schools are one big "advanced section" because nearly all their students are academically talented. Within some of these all-academic public schools, there are still *further advanced* groups along with the "regulars." In some schools the advanced or honors students in a grade move together through the day, "advanced" in all their courses. In other schools students are grouped differently in the various subject areas. Electives provide still more variety in grouping. Some electives, like the fourth year of a foreign language, are by their nature "advanced sections," because only the very capable students want them. Special courses like typing or shorthand can bring many different kinds of abilities and interests into a classroom. Some schools have certain courses designed to bring the widest possible spread of student perspectives and abilities into each section. The same schools, however, may have special college preparatory and advanced sections in other courses.

In the midst of the various attempts to meet the current demand for advanced standing for bright high school people, some common feelings about the *social* effects of ability grouping are emerging. Many students were quick to mention some of the disadvantages involved. Apparently all is not calm and peaceful within the advanced sections. One boy expressed his ambivalent feeling this way: "It's wonderful to be with these people, and you make friendships that are terribly important. Yet, at the same time, we are out to cut each other's throats on marks, scholarships, and college admissions. We have to be."

The competition was cherished—yet regretted. Some of the other comments were:

"It's terrifically stimulating."

"It keeps everyone on the ball."

"You can't get bored."

The vicious aspect of the competition was portrayed by this half-joking advice that had made its rounds in the school: "If someone's absent and calls you to get the homework, don't give it to him. Or give it wrong. Then he'll look stupid tomorrow and you'll look good!"

Whenever this topic arose in a discussion, students disagreed on just how serious it was. As two boys said: "It's not all that bad. We play along with each other—you know—help each other out on cramming— that kind of thing—there's a good relationship really."

In some schools the various sections formed virtually closed corporations. Advanced students said they usually ate lunch together and associated with each other in their social life. Some admitted they felt guilty about this. As one boy put it:

I find I even talk differently when I'm with some groups in school or out in the neighborhood—sort of like a split personality—you have to play two roles. You can't go telling them all about this intellectual-drive stuff.

[Another student picked up this idea.] I find it pretty hard to keep my friendships back in my neighborhood because so much of what we do together in this group doesn't seem to go with the people back there. I find it harder and harder to talk with them—harder and harder even to care what they think.

Some of these advanced students were quick to joke about themselves as separated from the "clods and unwashed multitudes," as one called them. Still, they were critical about this separation, sometimes welcoming it, sometimes seeing themselves as hiding in it, sometimes yearning to break out of it.

One teacher spoke up vehemently about what she called "ignoring the by-products of advanced sectioning." She stressed that the idea of challenging able students was important, and that putting the most capable of them together was part of the answer. She emphasized "part" as she spoke, and continued: "I have been appalled at the assumption that putting all the smartest students together and giving them more work to do would solve the problem of students not learning enough fast enough. There are some hazards. Strasbourg geese *do* have the biggest livers."

I must have looked puzzled. She went on:

Some advanced-placement classes stuff the students very much the way that geese are stuffed on the *pâté de foie gras* farms. And some of the consequences are not so good. It isn't that the plan is wrong—it's that wisdom is needed in carrying it out, in picking the right kind of teachers to do the job, in choosing the best approach to *learning and thinking* in those classes. And then there's the divisive element that is introduced. Advanced placement is only one of the divisive factors—there are a lot in this school—but we need to watch out for this one particularly, and somehow manage to have the advantages of sectioning without the disadvantages. Surely this should be possible.

The problem of *divisions* within a school—vocational *vs.* academic, advanced *vs.* regular, etc.—is one that Dr. James Conant emphasized in his report on the American high school.* How can we give individuals the advantages of specialized training without placing excessive restrictions on their associations with each other? Dr. Conant suggested that comprehensive high schools offer a senior-year course in Problems in Democracy which would *not* be sectioned according to ability or on the basis of college or vocational plans. The next school I visited had such a course in operation.

* James B. Conant, *The American High School Today*. New York: McGraw-Hill, 1959.

CHAPTER 21

A HIGH SCHOOL
THAT IS REALLY COMPREHENSIVE

It's the *spirit* around here that counts!

One of thirty boys in a mechanical drawing class was trying to put his finger on what he valued most in his high school experience. His school was a mid-western comprehensive high school of about eighteen hundred students. His classmates in this senior group were sitting on their stools behind their drafting desks. The room was large, and I had to move around a good deal to see the boys' faces when they spoke. I asked for some explanation of this "spirit." Answers came quickly:

Take the competition in this class. We are proud of these drawings. They get put up on the wall—we get graded on them—we like to see them really good. I mean it's good for us and it's good for the class.

A lot of it is because we're on our own. Each guy is in here for three hours, working on his own. You'll see some guys helping others who work slower or are on some different kind of thing.

I asked if this competition ever got to the throat-cutting stage. They laughed and gave these replies:

We're headed for jobs. Mr. Gullen will be placing most of us next year. If we're doing our best and laying out good work, there isn't much reason for cutting each other's throats.

Maybe the point is that we like this stuff and we're pretty good at it. It's a guy's own business, what he's learning.

So far these vocational boys had said nothing about the college preparatory students, or about college at all. Rather than raise questions, I thought I would wait to see what happened. This class had already proved to be a startling contrast to the vocational groups I had met in the other schools, where they had been so eager to talk about their relationship to the college-bound students. These boys wanted to talk about their own class and its "spirit":

"A lot of things help. The Junior Show is one thing. This really gets everybody in a big class together."

I had heard this before, even to the use of "everybody." But in many schools "everybody" turned out to be a handful of leaders and their friends. I asked these boys just who "everybody" was.

Everybody. We had six hundred juniors tied up with that show one way or another. We got forty on the stage, but backstage or making costumes, arranging sets and lighting, preparing the programs, writing the words and music—we really *did* have everybody.

No one in the room denied it. And the same description came later from the seniors in a special college preparatory class in English composition.

The boys recognized that the spirit they valued so much had many sources. They mentioned the clubs, the councils that planned out-of-school social events, homeroom representation in the student council, and—with great stress—"the way the counselors help you pick the right courses." They also spoke up strongly for their teachers:

The teachers are important in this school. Most of them are sincerely interested in us.

[Another boy picked this up quickly.] It isn't just an eight-hour job for them. We know we can go to a teacher and get help or just talk.

The teachers'll get in there and fight for you.

I was scheduled for another class at the end of this hour, but these boys wanted to go right ahead. One of them said, "We're good for another couple of hours on all this!" We were indeed, but I deferred to the schedule.

It was exciting to see people so enthusiastic about their school and their own role in it. Their teacher told me afterwards that a number of these boys would be going on to some further training, though more than half would not. He had asked me earlier if I wanted a show of hands on which ones were going on, but I had asked him not to bother. From the discussion, I could not guess which ones were headed for college.

PRIDE IN THE SCHOOL

The twenty college-bound seniors in a composition class didn't talk about the "spirit" of this school. Instead they spoke of "pride in the school" as the outstanding feature of their experience during the past three years. Here are some of their remarks:

The school's good scholastic reputation gives us all a good feeling.

Have you heard our band? Our choir? Our school orchestra does stuff that symphony orchestras do. This makes people proud, whether they belong to them or not.

You know Benny Goodman was upstairs visiting the band this morning? He was there most of the morning—it was really terrific! The band director figured that, since Goodman gets $17,000 for fifteen minutes on the Ed Sullivan show, we had about $80,000 worth of his time!

A lot is in our leaders—the kind of interest and enthusiasm they have.

These students, too, spoke about teachers who cared about them, teachers they could talk to as people. They also cited class activities that "brought everyone in." I still don't quite understand how this was accomplished, but I never found a dissenter among all the students I met at this school. The discussion ended with this:

I think a lot of the change in each of us is caused by our relationships here in school—with people in our class as well as with teachers.

Somehow the people we meet and the things we do here help us to find out more and more about the kind of people we are.

That's it—the thing that really happens as you go through this school is that you get to know yourself better.

WHERE ARE THE BARRIERS?

Most of the students in this school seemed to respect what they were doing and felt they "belonged" in the life of the school. An alert and vigorous boy spoke up for ". . . the kind of incentive I got when I knew I was going to college."

A minute later the boy next to him said: "I found that I really 'got going' in the course in electricity. Once I started in there I knew that I'd found something I wanted to do and was good at. The rest of the school looked better to me then, even though I still don't get much out of sitting in history class."

It would be easy to account for the lack of barriers in this school by saying that the pressures are different in this part of the country. It is true that the desire for admission to Eastern prestige colleges is not strong here. Last year about two-fifths of the graduating class in this school went on to four-year colleges, including some thirty-six different institutions with a wide range of challenges and opportunities. None of those students went to West Coast or East Coast colleges. But back at the comprehensive high school where Mr. Smith was teaching, where the college preparatory students and "shop kids" lived in isolation from each other, the students weren't suffering from prestige-college pressure, either.

The crux of the situation here, beyond the teachers' concern and interest, seemed to me to be this: the school's schedule is set up course-by-course, not by "tracks" or separate curricula. Vocational students, business students, and college prep students are not assigned to separate compartments.

A PROGRAM FOR EACH INDIVIDUAL

Fifteen years ago this school had twelve separate curricula: three in college preparation, one in general, one in home economics, three in industrial training, and four in business training. Now, as an administrator explained, "the courses are scheduled for the individual." This sounds simple, and most schools would subscribe to the idea if it were feasible. It is feasible in this Midwestern school because the community is intensely interested in education. Every year about a thousand of the eighteen hundred students attend the summer school. A college-bound girl who wants to take shorthand or her senior history course in the summer can do so and thereby open up her schedule for the next year. Or a boy with scientific interests could do what one of the boys in the drawing class told me he had done: finished his senior English course in the summer so he could take chemistry in his final year, along with his vocational courses and the required history courses.

The grip of The Schedule, so often the major block to objectives that seem most ideal in school planning, is loosened in this school. One teacher explained:

This summer program is not just something for people who have failed or are weak in a subject. Last summer less than two hundred of the thousand students who came were trying to pass off a course they had failed. The others had a special interest in certain courses, or had planned their next year in such a way that they needed to complete certain requirements in the summer.

An administrator stressed the serious approach of the students to the summer program:

The summer session includes 40 full days. It runs six days a week, and classes begin at 7 A.M. We offer the things that are in demand. We put in an advanced chemistry course, beginning Spanish, art, engineering drawing, and second-year Latin last summer, along with most of the previous summer's program. We had seven sections of junior history last summer—they alone drew more than two hundred students.

I asked him what he thought were the reasons for so many students coming to school in the summer. Didn't job opportunities pull many of them away from summer study?

Well, it may be that there aren't many jobs these students can get here just for the summer. But I think a lot has to do with things these people want to take: choir, advanced-standing courses, typing, the art workshop, the Bible as literature, and bookkeeping. These students, wherever they're headed, want to take a lot more than they can fit into the regular school year.

[Another teacher added:] Remember that activities like playing in the orchestra or what we call "cadet teaching" for potential teachers, come right into the day's schedule. If a kid wants to do those things, he has to make his plans so he can carry his requirements too.

[A guidance counselor explained:] A boy could be good in tenth-grade engineering drawing and do well in advanced geometry, but a separate vocational or college prep "track" might force him out of one of these courses. Our ideal is *to build the strongest possible program for each student,* and then arrange, with the help of the summer program, to schedule it.

GROUPING STUDENTS

The whole range of students is included in the eleventh- and twelfth-grade history sections. English sections are arranged according to ability. Academic electives, such as regular or advanced courses in science or foreign languages, automatically get the more able students—probably college-bound, but not necessarily. Other electives, such as shorthand and bookkeeping, include both college-bound *and* vocational students. And people involved in the band, choir, orchestra, or studio arts take these as regular courses, whatever the rest of their program includes.

In this way a vocation-minded student is sure to encounter *in actual classes* college-bound students, who may or may not be brighter than he is. A college-bound student may be working ahead in an advanced chemistry course or a special English literature course with some of his classmates who are not headed for college. He will surely be studying "problems in democracy" with students who are not college-minded, who may be a lot slower than he is *or who may be brighter*. But he will meet "those others" in serious discussion, not just on the ball field or in the brass section.

Arguments have been advanced against Dr. Conant's recommendation that a comprehensive high school should have a problems in democracy course that cuts across the lines of the students' abilities and their college or vocational plans. Teachers have said, for example, that you cannot give a high-powered course under such conditions. But, as one teacher in this school commented: "What's to prevent the school from offering, at other points in the schedule, elective history courses which *are* high powered, *in addition* to the required problems in democracy course which comes in the senior year?"

One other obvious criticism has been made: The suggested problems in democracy course cannot require intensive reading and writing assignments. The answer is that it can still be intelligent and challenging in the kind of experience it provides for the "mixed" sections. It *is* harder to teach a mixed section. One history teacher in this school explained:

Certainly it's easier if all your students are bright and talk the academic language. It's easier if they are fast and able readers, too. I admit I have many moments when I find this mixed section in history hard going. There are times when the brightest get restless and when the slowest get lost. But if the teacher really wants to make it work he can. Assignments can be individualized—certainly I have my strongest students doing a lot beyond the basic minimum. But there are many important things these heterogeneous sections *need* to discuss with each other and *can* discuss with real profit. And these things have to do with history—they don't provide just a social exchange.

IS IT JUST A QUESTION OF SCHEDULING?

The healthy state of the social relationships and high morale I found in this school are surely not just the result of course-scheduling and a widely supported summer session, much as these allow students to have fuller and more varied programs. Rather, this type of scheduling and the summer work seem to be *results* of the school's and community's inspired attitudes. Those attitudes seem to include the desires to improve *the relationships of students of varied abilities and destinations and to meet the need for a strong, appropriate program for each student.* These two goals do not necessarily conflict. Too often, they are discussed in public controversy as though they were mutually exclusive. Sometimes neither one is considered a respectable concern, and we are told the real issue is that of social coddling *vs.* academic pounding in the space-age battle for survival. If that is the major issue, then quite out-of-the-mainstream is the boy who said, "I think a lot of the change in each of us is caused by our relationships here in school—with people in our classes as well as with teachers."

PART SEVEN
Values in Growing Up

CHAPTER 22
THE INTANGIBLE SPIRIT

But it's different for a City High girl!

It certainly was, if I were to judge from one girl's description of her former school. I will call her new school City High. It is an all-academic, public school for sixteen hundred girls who come from all parts of a large city. Just how was it "different for a City High girl"? I got the first inkling when I sat and talked with one of the guidance counselors the first morning of my visit. Our conversation was interrupted when the telephone rang and she answered it: "All right, Mrs. Gatling, we'll see you on Thursday at 10 o'clock, then."

She returned the telephone to the holder, laughed, and turned to me again. We chatted a few moments. Then she pointed to the telephone.

That was a mother, a graduate of this school. Her daughter is having a very hard time of it here academically and is already down a grade. But the girl seems determined to fight it out and stay in the school. I told her mother it was a stiff challenge for her daughter and perhaps she should consider sending her to her neighborhood school. The mother said, "Mrs. McCann, I don't care whether she spends ten years in the tenth grade. I want her to stay at City High and learn to be a lady!"

The objective of "learning how to be a lady" was something of a surprise to me. The school's reputation to outsiders centered on high-powered academic work. I also was suspicious of mass efforts to develop "manners." Superficial? Even hypocritical? I wondered. I soon found that the girls and teachers at City High have developed a serious, direct approach to matters of personal development and behavior. The phrase I kept hearing while I was there was "the intangible spirit of City High." The students used this phrase with many different meanings. This became clear to me the very first day, when I sat in the lunch room for three successive periods and talked to everyone who entered. Girls gathered around the tables and joined in eagerly:

129

In this school you don't see cliques or castes of people in one religion or race like you do in junior high school.

Yes, that's the *best* thing about City High!

In junior high we felt the teachers expected us to be bad and were watching us until we *were* bad. So we were bad! Here they seem to expect us to behave well, so we do.

Here you have a chance to see people do the thing they do well—arts, sports, studies, committee work. When you see people doing their special thing well, you get to know them and tend to get away from having bad feelings about them.

Prejudice is something that comes from the home. But here someone coming in with prejudice finds that it just doesn't go and that people who have that attitude are looked down on. So they eventually give up their prejudice no matter what went on in their homes.

You hear a lot about "City High Girls don't do that!" You get a little sick of this sometimes, and people kid about it some, but it does mean a lot —as if some kind of tradition were pushing us upwards.

You really learn manners here. I don't know—it seems to be passed on from the older classes to the younger ones. Younger girls see the way the older ones behave—kinds of courtesy they show, the way they speak. This is something that is "done" and the younger kids adapt to it and become part of it.

It's funny to see the way neighborhood sororities and gangs drop off as far as the City High girls are concerned. In junior high you need something to belong to that makes you feel important. You also need something for protection in some neighborhoods and some schools: my-gang-can-beat-up-your-gang, of if-you-hurt-me-my-gang-will-get-you. But here at City High the biggest appeal of the neighborhood sororities is to the 9A girls who are new and don't know anybody. By the time you get in 9B you don't have this need. The school itself is something to belong to.

You don't see teachers patrolling around the lunch room, do you? We take care of that, and all study periods up in the auditorium, too. And if a teacher is late or doesn't show up in class, the elected student chairman for the section takes over. She runs the class and gives the assignment; if she doesn't do well, the class disciplines her. It's like a very good democracy—you feel you have a place.

I was struck by the idea of everybody having some responsibility. I had often heard of this in other schools—from students who easily won elections whenever they ran for office. I asked, "How about the person who is *not* a committee chairman or a group coordinator?" The answer: "Well, then *that* person's the assistant!"

With this flood of eager comment, I wondered if perhaps some students in the school might not share this enthusiasm. I even asked in some desperation, "What about the person who, for her own reasons, just doesn't get into this spirit? Isn't there anyone who fights it?" The answer that came first was this: "*People don't seem to do that. They figure that if they hurt the school they hurt themselves, since they have so much say in running the school.*"

One girl had the final word after the bell had rung at the end of the last of the lunch periods. She gathered her books together and came back, evidently determined to make this point clear to me:

I came to City High for the schooling. I didn't care about the other stuff. I thought that the pledge, the oath, the Code of Courtesy was all so much nonsense. But I've really changed my thinking about this. It begins to be a part of you when you live with it so long. You find that you really *have* responsibility and are being trained for leadership—and all of a sudden you can take it!

TEN GIRLS AND THE PRINCIPAL

I was standing in the main office waiting to talk with the principal of the school when I saw two girls run up to her. I was near enough to hear what they were saying, and what I saw and heard in the next half hour is the kind of thing which, multiplied a thousand times over, shapes the morale of a school. One of the two girls, a Negro, explained that an integration march was scheduled for the next week in Washington. Students from all the East Coast states were going to take part. Her friend, who was white, asked if they might organize a school group, and if the principal would help them. I watched the principal as the two girls talked and noticed how she listened with extraordinary care.

Her listening went beyond mere courtesy. I saw this again a little later when she met with these two girls and eight others. She had phoned the president of the Board of Education and had been told that individuals could go on this march, but they were not to claim to represent the school. This was difficult to explain to these girls. They were excited and impatient. The board's ruling seemed evasive, even cowardly to them. They were ready for a fight. I watched the principal absorb some of this resentment. As she did so, she asked searching questions about what the girls knew about the march, what kind of planning they would need to do before going, what kind of contribution they wanted to make. There was nothing patronizing in her attitude, and the girls also seemed to listen carefully and think. Their thoughtfulness and eagerness, it seemed, were being *dignified* by the principal's questions and by her attention to their answers. The atmosphere was a little like that in a living room where a discerning hostess was drawing out her guests on a subject that urgently concerned them all.

The girls had arrived in the conference room in an uproar of unfocused zeal. They seemed to be leaving it with a good deal more understanding of their own motives, the board's position, and their own role as people concerned about a national problem.

Those who say that "values are caught, not taught," could indeed point to the principal's handling of this meeting and say, "There it is. That's what I mean." The whole tradition and practice of the school seems to be interwoven with this idea of "the intangible spirit." This principal is a person who has a great deal to do with it. Yet her influence in the school is an *expression* of this spirit as well as an inspiration for it.

ACTIVITIES THAT AMOUNT TO SOMETHING

The school's non-academic activities looked to me fairly standard on paper. Where they did not seem standard was in the many ways the students were given genuine responsibility. Responsibility was expected in the auditorium, study halls, the cafeteria, even in classrooms at the start of each period when a teacher was late or absent. The teacher in charge of school activities—I will call her Mrs. Swarthout—was the kind who was willing to work twenty-four hours a day for the good of the students, just as was the man who had the leadership class in one of the schools I had visited earlier. Here again was someone who *gave dignity* to work on a newspaper, or interest in a student council project—dignity to a student trying to carry out her responsibility in organizing a class party, or to a group working to bring the school into community service. She hoped to stretch the students as far as possible in the *kind* of responsibility they could take and in ways that counted to them. She explained: "I try to make sure the girls see the three different areas of responsibility—those of the school administration, of the faculty, and of the students themselves. You can't play at this and pretend the girls are responsible where they are really not. You couldn't possibly get away with it anyway. They'd see through it in a minute!"

She was also constantly on the lookout to find opporunities for service, contribution, or creative action from students who weren't in the midst of things in school. I heard about this often from shy, appreciative students who felt "worth something around school." As one girl said, "What Mrs. Swarthout really does is to make us see our own possibilities as people. You get some idea about what you can do when someone like her *cares* and is willing to let you go out on a limb."

The image of another student flashed into my mind. I vividly recalled the boy in the composition class in the Middle West, the boy who said, "Through the things that happen around here you get to *know* yourself better."

Mrs. Swarthout devotes all her time to student activities, except for one class of her own. This work, as I had seen in other schools, requires far more than "full time" if the school is serious about genuine responsibility for its students. Results like those at City High are not likely to be obtained if the person in charge is indifferent or unimaginative. But even though he is admirably suited to meet the challenge, he will have a hard time doing any thing impressive if he must struggle in a sea of clerical work, heavy classroom teaching, coaching, and committee work.

A teacher such as Mrs. Swarthout is not regarded as a "nice extra" in this school. She clearly represents a major part of the experience the school offers. This is worth emphasizing, since City High is geared for ambitious academic effort and has a tradition of high academic achievement. There is no rift here between academic standards and participation in school activities.

ANOTHER TRADITION

In this same high school, the responsibility for welcoming the new students into the 9A class is carried seriously by a large group of seniors. They stay with a homeroom and seem to go well beyond the perfunctory "any problems?" approach. Many of the younger students told how much they appreciated the understanding and interest of the seniors who made it their business to help launch the freshmen in the school.

I saw a set of letters to the principal, required of senior sponsors at certain points in the year. I was startled by the perceptiveness of many of these letters, and by the imagination the girls showed in dealing with problems of personal and group morale.

One faculty member noted that these student efforts in passing along certain standards to incoming classes had special value for new teachers as well:

If a new teacher will keep her mouth shut and listen for a while, she'll learn a good deal about the school from watching its seniors in action, explaining the values and traditions of City High. When I came here, I found I had to change completely my former approach to the students. These girls are so responsible, yet so tactful in dealing with new students and teachers! I have never known of a case where the girls took advantage of a new teacher or of a weak or shy teacher or substitute.

A SCHOOL'S COMMITMENT

City High's sixteen hundred students are all girls. Readers may wonder if it is fair to put such emphasis on these signs of morale in a public school which is not comprehensive and not even coeducational. The *expression* of morale in the comments quoted here from students and teachers might stem from the fact that the school enrolls only girls. But it would hardly be fair to jump to the conclusion that boys have a monopoly on selfishness, apathy, cynicism, and ruthless competition. I found evidences of especially high morale in more than this one school, as this book shows. The "intangible spirit of City High" seems to me to tell a good deal more than the fact that girls can achieve a strong morale when no boys are around. Someone could probably find examples of the opposite spirit in another all-girl school, and account for the poor morale with the same notion that "that's what happens when you educate girls separately."

Surely the distinctive signs of good morale I saw in schools other than this one show that "the intangible spirit" has no fixed pattern or required ingredient. Remember the students in the vocational drawing class who talked about their pride in their work, the girls who broke down the social barriers between the desirables and the untouchables, the student president who was working on a better basis for choosing leaders, the "shop kids'" insistence that I must see Mr. Smith teach, the lunch table where it was "all right" to talk about religion as well as baseball—each of these examples is drawn from a different school, none claiming to have the last word on morale.

It seems to come down to a school's commitment: just what things it cares about, and then what kind of imagination and effort it calls into action. A faculty member at City High spoke this way about one idea of a school's commitment:

Certainly we're interested in the human part of education—very much interested. In fact, that's one of the reasons for having this kind of school. These girls have real ability, and if they weren't able to use it, all kinds of problems would develop. So our biggest job is helping them all to use the ability they have. That, in turn, makes them better and happier people.

This reference to the students' "ability" applied, obviously, to their ability to function *as persons,* not just to their ability to handle words and numbers. She stressed this: *"We don't hover over them. We do try to set the stage for them to grow. We try to convince them that we are interested in seeing them grow and in how they grow."*

It was only a few minutes later that I heard a little eleventh-grader say really the same thing, but from the other side of the front office. Anxious to add one more thing to what we were talking about together this morning, the girl said:

What I was trying to tell you was this: I like to be in the center of things. I will *never* be a sheep. I used to be pretty nasty. People were always criticizing me. But this year I think I'm really better. The other day Miss Lansbury said to me that I'm growing up, and I felt so good—even though I know I'm not grown up yet!

CHAPTER 23

STUDENTS IN THE WORLD BEYOND SCHOOL

Are high school students indifferent to the realities of community and world affairs? Are apathy and neutrality the dominant attitudes of young people coming into our adult society? My experience on this venture leads me to give a vehement "No!" to these questions, despite the recurrence of statements to the contrary in some of the recent portrait-of-a-generation literature. It is true that I often saw a protective, surface apathy when discussions were "just verbal," as one girl characterized them, but awareness and concern were unmasked quickly when certain students cut through the verbalisms and took advantage of opportunities to react and to think.

One of my approaches involved putting on the blackboard the names of the people in public life whom the students said they admired most. I had asked a number of groups to do this, mainly to see what names recurred. I also asked for a list of "most-admired" people. Usually current political names would quickly fill both lists. Standard target names (Khrushchev, Nasser) kept reappearing on the "least-admired" side. "Sophisticated" groups would try to stay away from names that would mark them as gullible or naive. Some spoke up earnestly for Dr. Salk and Dr. Schweitzer. In most groups, students showed a competitive spirit in determining which names would go into which column. On the whole, though, this proved to be little more than a word game for the students. I found various signs of sharp contrasts in student awareness of the world beyond school. Two significant examples follow. The first shows two radically different types of attitudes of school newspapers toward community and world affairs. The other shows a group of students speaking out vigorously about their vision of the future and their role in it.

FIT TO PRINT

A school newspaper can reveal certain student and school interests very clearly. Notice the range of interests suggested by this set of headlines in one school paper:

1. SCHOOL GIVES UNESCO CHECK TO UNITED NATIONS DELEGATES (the largest headline). A picture and article describe the ceremony in which two students presented the money collected to UN delegates, one from Ceylon and one from India.
2. JUNIOR COLLEGE TO OPEN SOON. A discussion of a new community college.
3. ESSAYISTS TO DISCUSS REVOLUTION LEADER AND UNITED NATIONS. A report of a coming social studies project.
4. TWO BANDS AT FETE. SCHOOL FUNDS EARNED. An item on a recent dance and plans for a coming one.
5. MARTIN AND SIROZ RECEIVE TOP MARKS: ALL ABOVE 85 ON LAST TERM'S HONOR ROLL. The article included full-face pictures of the boy and girl receiving top marks.
6. THREE CLASSES TO TOUR HISTORY MUSEUM
7. LITERATURE CLUB FORMED TO DISCUSS GREAT BOOKS
8. GERMAN PUPILS VIEW MOVIE AND NEWSREEL
9. ESSAY CONTEST STRESSES THEME OF NEGRO HISTORY

I found a serious, well-written article below each of these headlines. A number of these articles gave evidence of the students' mature interest in the world beyond the school. Illustrations of their interest and related activities were given earlier in this report.

"CONTROVERSIAL ISSUES ARE OUT!"

In another school the student editor told me rather bitterly, "Frankly, the editorial board is hard-put to find things to publish in the paper! Controversial issues are out! Well, the Board of Education won't allow us to go on record on anything controversial—the paper goes into libraries and homes all over the city."

I asked for some examples of past incidents that had made his editorial board so wary of dealing with anything beyond the Senior Hop in the

138 HIGH SCHOOL STUDENTS SPEAK OUT

paper. He thought a minute, then replied, "Well, I heard that about ten years ago some kid wrote an editorial about the teachers and the whole issue was suppressed." He noticed that this seemed pretty long ago. Also, he seemed to recognize that the incident probably did not justify the continued indifference or wariness of the paper's staff. He went on:

"Last year a boy wrote an article on the H-bomb tests, saying they should be stopped. The faculty adviser said he'd have to have an article in there on the other side, too, just to show that the paper recognized both sides. The boy resigned—what can you do?"

I wondered if in this particular case the faculty adviser might not have been used as an excuse for apathy. No doubt the climate of the school had considerable effect here, too. Yet couldn't the paper help *create* a new climate, and not simply reflect the one that existed?

This editor seemed intelligent and thoughtful. He was alert and mature in his talk about plans for college and the subjects that interested him. But the newspaper, to him, seemed to be just something to get out by Friday with all the pages filled. The real business of school for his schoolmates and himself was, according to him, "fighting it out for admission to the right colleges. Those scores are everything!"

Surely one good reason for having a school newspaper can be to help students reach beyond the walls of their school. Yet the fact that a student has served as editor of the school paper, supposedly so impressive on college application blanks, evidently may mean little more than that the student has had practice meeting deadlines, assembling, pasting, and proofreading.

"THE INDIVIDUAL DOES MATTER!"

Perhaps the most heartening discussion about the world beyond the school walls that I witnessed took place in a history class of high-powered students. One boy had tipped me off beforehand that it might be interesting to ask the students which period in history they would most like to have lived in. I tried this approach, and the class eagerly took up the idea.

It soon became clear to me that some of the students were mainly interested in deducing what the answers revealed about the personalities of their classmates. But others concentrated on the idea of the individual's importance and responsibility at *any* given point in history. They kept choosing either the present or some time in the future as the moment in history they would like to occupy, reaching on up to "being the first pioneer to arrive on the moon." They gradually developed the idea that *a person* is of crucial importance, capable of affecting the whole history of mankind. They drew examples from their reading—ranging from science fiction stories of prehistoric times to *War and Peace*—from their visions of different kinds of Utopias, and from television programs they had seen. They seemed to be creating a "platform" they wanted to stand on, and they showed excitement and eagerness in the creating. The "platform" was simply that a person *did* count, *was* responsible, not necessarily for moral or religious reasons, but simply for reasons of fact: an individual could be the determining factor in the role of discoverer, the instigator, the peace-maker, or the leader.

These students were unusually articulate and alert. Many of them held top positions of responsibility in an "activities-minded" school. They spoke seriously about the current trend of apathy in the colleges and of "forces working against the individual." They kept speaking of such books as *1984, Brave New World,* and *The Organization Man,* which many of them had read on their own. Yet they displayed sincere belief in the potential importance of each individual to mankind, and they expressed this view earnestly and enthusiastically. Their enthusiasm seemed to me to be well based in conviction, not wishful thinking, in a sense of personal responsibility, not egocentricity.

This was the school where the students stressed "We talk about things in English and history here." The independent reading, the student leadership, the naturalness about "talking about things in class" are surely a part of the story. But regardless of what accounts for the spirit of world-mindedness of these students, the spirit was there in that room.

Some of the comments I heard from high school students during my visits were discouraging and some were heartening. But much of the talk and action I have tried to describe suggests that some schools fully recognize the important potentialities of their students in their role as maturing, thoughtful, responsible citizens. Those schools do more than provide projects to keep their students busy. They seek, and find, ways of relating courses to student interests, professed values to student actions. The opportunities they offer their students for shouldering responsibility bring out more than the "pathetically solemn efforts to talk so importantly about so little," on which one boy was quoted earlier. These schools do not find that it is either necessary or appropriate to separate academic and vocational work from "what really matters to their students."

The extraordinary potentialities of our present high school population as developing citizenry might well be examined when adult citizens assemble for roundtable talks or TV panel discussions on education and when school boards meet to consider ways of making the school experience more challenging. The challenge the students need cannot be offered solely through more textbooks, more homework, and harder marking systems. As one high school girl said to me, "A chance for some responsibility in school or around town shouldn't have to be some kind of extra, sort of on a par with the chess club or the band."

What I saw in my visits to the schools leads me to believe that one simple way of getting constructive action and thought from high school students is to let them know that it is expected of them and allow them ample opportunities to show it. We might find that under such conditions students will readily use their reserves of creativity, imagination, and energy. Perhaps then fewer students would feel the way the one boy did when he said to me:

"You have the feeling you're just waiting around to grow up. But you get tired of just doing the homework part of the time and living it up as a teen-ager the rest of the time. I think a lot of us would like to have *something more*—but what is there?"

PART   EIGHT
Perspectives

CHAPTER 24

AN EMERGING PICTURE

I guess most teachers and school heads don't have much idea of these feelings and ideas we've been talking about. Maybe some of them would be interested in knowing about them—maybe some wouldn't. Your study makes me believe that some people think it's worth finding out what *we* think our time in high school is like. But look—you're a teacher—how are you going to walk into your own classroom again after all you've been hearing in these schools?

The eleventh-grader who said this seemed well aware of the challenge he was putting to me. I am conscious of his challenge as I look back on my visits. Faces and voices of many hundreds of high school people remain clear in my memory. I rather expected these faces to become blurred, forming a landscape full of merging details. I now find quite the opposite: the details are more insistent than the whole picture. Yet a picture does emerge.

In describing this picture as I see it, I will *not* try to make a portrait of the typical American high school student or his school. The aim of this study has been to examine the effects of school experiences on student values in a few schools. Broad generalizations based on the findings are precluded because the sampling of schools is small and by no means nationally representative. Furthermore, the students who spoke out in this study expressed a wide variety of views and opinions, showing that they do not readily conform to a teen-age stereotype. Instead of trying to form a composite profile, I will attempt to summarize the comments given by the students in each of six areas. This may help the reader to gain a perspective of all the voices, impressions, and experiences that have been described.

CURRICULUM

In some schools I heard little, if any, spontaneous reference to the curriculum. The experiences which seemed to matter most to students in their own growing-up were described mainly as happening outside

143

of school—with friends, jobs, new responsibilities. In other cases, the curriculum was something discussed solely in relation to a determined drive toward an anxiously sought payment in the form of marks. For some students, those marks "were" the curriculum. Some students even described the curriculum as unreal and irrelevant to any of their own concerns, motives, or interests. Examples were given, however, of courses which awakened or challenged what the students believed was their developing vision of themselves and their world.

In virtually all discussions of curriculum, students of widely ranging abilities and aims stressed the need to be able to see some point, some purpose in a course's work. Even those enrolled in the most high-powered courses made hardly any comment about the *amount* of homework, even when it required three or more hours a night and more on weekends.

The students seemed to be most concerned about having to do some course work which was meaningless from their point of view. The courses they singled out for expressions of appreciation were those that made them feel they were taking an active part in the subjects they were studying. Apparently, they did not like to feel that they were just maneuvering answers without having an opportunity to explore, speculate, and come to grips with the subject.

Students in advanced-standing classes were particularly urgent about the need for flexibility and challenge in intellectual exploration. Many of them felt trapped in advanced courses which just required *more* of the patterned, superficial, question-and-answer work that they had criticized in regular academic classes. On the other hand, a problem arose when departments offered work of higher quality and with more stimulating materials in the advanced courses. If this occurred, students in regular courses often felt that the more human, interesting materials (as in the English work with *Death of a Salesman* and *Babbitt*) that were offered to advanced sections would be just as valuable for regular sections, and would be as appropriate to them as the standard fare (*Silas Marner* and *A Tale of Two Cities*), or more so. Some students in regular sections felt that the real challenge to think and to explore was reserved for the advanced sections, and that teachers assumed that the regular sections had no interest or enthusiasm for anything beyond lesson-learning.

Students were divided about what to respect in a course. Some courses that provided a lot of hard work on the learn-the-answer level seemed "better" than those involving more flexibility of organization and more study of problems with solutions which were less readily available, such as certain courses in problems of democracy. This caused a conflict if some students found their major challenge and interest was in a course which was looked down on by teachers or by students as less "respectable."

The same problem of status appeared occasionally where schools provided unusual opportunities in the arts, a particularly strong choir, or a challenging dramatics program, for example. The academically respectable courses sometimes challenged the prestige of serious work in these fields or tended to create an aura of superficiality about work in the arts which was actually of genuine quality.

Individual exploration in a subject field often appeared as an extra, something to do if the required work was done. Students spoke of the required work as simply time-consuming, with little or no individual challenge to explore *within* assignments and little opportunity or encouragement to go beyond them. Students who did go beyond the regular work sometimes spoke of this as if they considered it unrelated to the uniform requirements of a course. For example, I heard many discussions of individual reading, but the students usually said that the books they read on their own rarely became a part of any curricular discussion or research. Still, those books often represented considerable intellectual challenge beyond the curricular fare. Students spoke up eagerly in support of courses that did allow for flexibility in reading and assignment, individual research, and student share in planning.

TEACHING AND TEACHERS

Teachers were a favorite topic in the interviews. They were discussed with remarkably little personal griping or idolizing, but with efforts to identify personal approaches and professional techniques that the students felt were important in teaching. Many students seemed to see good teaching as something that transcended the subject rather than as something that illuminated it. A teacher's personality was often a focus for discussion, but the students were willing to move beyond personality into an evaluation of effective or ineffective teaching.

Great variety in viewpoints about teachers' classroom techniques ap-

peared. These themes recurred: the need for teachers to build confidence
in the students; to explain adequately; to open a subject up for exploration rather than simply present it; and to *allow* students, if not even to
challenge the teacher's statements, at least to think on their own rather
than just to accept or recite. Students resented having their exploring
and thinking cut off either by remarks such as "That's off the subject!"
or "We haven't time to go into that!"

Students urgently advocated student-teacher collaboration in identifying topics for research and for individual and group study. The picture
of adults determining, mimeographing, and lecturing on Questions of
Concern to Young People, without consultation with the persons most
involved, came in for some ironic comments. Capitalization of students' interests and abilities, or even the mere recognition of students as
people, was illustrated in a number of positive ways in certain teachers'
practice.

Student-teacher rapport outside of class seemed important to many
students. Many felt that such rapport, whether achieved in activities,
guidance, clubs, or individual conferences, had a great deal to do with
classroom morale and with the potential influence of teachers on the
school climate.

The idea of entering secondary school teaching as a career seemed to
many students unthinkable, even ridiculous or contemptible. These
students spoke of the teaching profession as requiring dreary repetition,
underpaid drudgery, and intellectual death. Other conversations, fewer
in number, revealed students who saw teaching in an idealistic light,
even though, for financial reasons or because of suspicion of the restrictions of "the system," they might still for themselves, reject the idea
of teaching.

Just how these images of the teaching profession developed was
described or implied in many comments. The image varied more from
school to school than within a single school. It varied with sex, also. A
large number of girls seemed to be planning for a teaching career, perhaps because of their own academic success and a feeling of being "at
home" in the school setting. Their over-all motivation was less clearly
articulated than that of the much smaller number of boys who were
motivated toward a teaching career.

When the small group of seniors in one of the schools experimented with teaching younger pupils, these seniors developed a better understanding of the learning process and the teacher's role in it. They became aware that self-discipline is necessary for teaching and for translating knowledge into action. The effect of this experience on the seniors' attitudes toward teaching as a career choice was not determined, however.

THE CRUSH FOR COLLEGE ADMISSION

In five of the eight schools, admission to college was crucially important, according to both students and teachers. Competition for marks appeared to be growing in intensity, incentive for individual exploration was becoming more and more restricted, student activities were being decreased or eliminated, and extreme nervous tension was often generated, all in the drive to Get into the Right College. These problems were accentuated by the drive to win scholarships, whether needed or not, for reasons of school or family prestige. Such driving pressure, described more than once as "a neurotic obsession with college admission," seemed to dominate the thinking of many students and to be the central motivation for their school efforts. Even certain extracurricular activities and school service programs became, for some, a college admissions maneuver.

This drive apparently could become so strong within a school that general and vocational students would speak of a lack in their own motivation, even a lack in *themselves*, since they did not have the college pressure to drive them. They regarded the college preparatory student with some envy, not because of the future advantages of a college education, but because of the single-minded purposes which college admission seemed to provide. On the other hand, most college preparatory students agreed that the effects of the intense competitiveness were undesirable. Some students caught in the "crush" spoke of ways of transcending it by themselves. Others spoke of the ways the school tried to help. Still others, outside of the orbit of preoccupation with prestige colleges, demonstrated the kinds of morale and achievement that can be attained when college admission pressures do not dominate a school.

THE NEED FOR RESPONSIBILITY

The present Teen-Age Culture has been portrayed from time to time in a stereotype of the adolescent. The much-publicized characteristics of apathy, rebelliousness, and irresponsibility associated with the stereotype were not present in all the schools I visited, though. In fact, the typical student charactertistics were quite the opposite in some instances.

While student responsibility was less *discussed* by students than were the curriculum, teachers, and college admissions, its presence or absence could be detected readily. The student government activities that were described ranged from busy-work to important action from the students' viewpoints. Sometimes the student government was permitted to encompass only those activities that adults considered safe. These activities usually offered little challenge to student initiative and effort. A few of the schools visited had evidently found effective ways of enlisting a large number of their students in meaningful responsibilities. How student concern developed and action resulted were demonstrated impressively.

The student's potential role in actual planning for a school, including its curriculum, was illustrated constructively in the case of seven seniors' self-initiated study of major aspects of their school. In this example, the whole matter of leadership, so much discussed on college application blanks, came in for some close examination with interesting results.

DIVISIVE FORCES IN THE SCHOOL AND COMMUNITY

In a school where social prejudice had been imported from the community, the students appeared to be deeply concerned, but they expressed grave doubts about their ability to break down established prejudice patterns once they themselves had become adults. Social division born within the school itself was apparent in certain high schools that exhibited signs of a split between college preparatory students and other students. Some schools revealed a similar cleavage between advanced and regular college preparatory sections. Efforts to bring about unity were described eloquently by some students. They were concerned with understanding the divisive forces and with discovering ways of meeting them—ways that schools, especially those designed to be "comprehensive," can work toward harmony and mutual respect within diversity.

VALUES AND GROWING UP

Can adults communicate through the wall which so often appears to surround the Teen-Age Culture? Can the school be more than simply the setting where students' values develop at random? Can it harness positive forces which will help to shape values? Answers to these questions, even though they were central to the goals of this study, can only be inferred from the samples of talk and behavior given in this report.

When they were faced with a request to compare their own concerns and outlook of three years ago with those of the present, the students responded thoughtfully and seriously. It is important to recognize that they disagreed on whether their schools had any relation to the changes which had occurred. Their self-examination stressed positive values. They sensed that the years had brought increased responsibility and growing independence. But were these the result of school encouragement? Only, apparently, in some schools. Elsewhere, the schools were seen as restrictive influences. Some of the schools permitted or fostered responsible thinking and action, but others appeared to exclude genuine freedom. Students pictured themselves as amenable to guidance, but hostile to indoctrination.

Public affairs did not often arise in the group conversations unless such topics were introduced by the visitor. When asked to name men and women most admired and least admired in public life, students generally gave names of headline political figures. The discussion of the names was generally superficial and indicated far less interest and information than did the discussion of the young people's individual development. Their own social relationships were, perhaps inevitably, a far more exciting topic for consideration than were public or community problems. But it is only fair to say that exceptions were found, and these were the more dramatic by contrast.

What relation does the social structure of a high school have to its scholastic organization? Are students who are strong academically numbered among the social outcasts? Some schools traditionally revere the athlete rather than the scholar. Where this is true, why is student government dominated by the college preparatory group? Students eagerly debated some of the inconsistencies of their own behavior.

What they talked *about* is less important than what they *said*. Their words revolved around dozens of concerns, and highlighted activities from school politics to religious retreats. Yet, because young people's growth in their teens is growth in and through school, what emerged can stand as a portrait of their schools. If they sometimes talked as if the school were a living entity, and spoke of its spirit as if it existed apart from themelves and their teachers, such a view merely intensifies one's impression of the significance of the whole experience. The spirit of the school *can* reach into the lives of its students, and this spirit and morale, the tradition and the values which the students reflect, carry the school into the world outside. The school which makes its students conscious primarily of marks and by-the-book recitation is one that projects a narrow image. The greater the vision of the school, the more it forces its students to be self-directing and responsible in every action of their lives. What the school teaches is what its graduates become.

CHAPTER 25

SOME PROFESSIONALS RESPOND

It is my impression that these high school students are speaking out of an underlying idealism. Some of the expressions of determination to succeed are most encouraging—for example the statement of the class president who said, "We've worked together to solve our problems and I think we shall continue to do so." What these young people need are schools with traditions based on more substantial foundations: "a tradition that is pushing us upwards," as the girl said of one school which has such a sense of purpose . . ."—DONALD A. ELDRIDGE, PRESIDENT OF BENNETT COLLEGE, CHAIRMAN, COMMITTEE ON SCHOOL AND COLLEGE RELATIONS OF THE EDUCATIONAL RECORDS BUREAU

Before I offer a concluding statement about my own observations, certain other voices should be heard, voices speaking from many different relationships—in teaching, administration, testing, and guidance—to school and college students in the educational adventure. The professional educators who are joined in the common concern which prompted this study have been a sounding board for the report of the results, and the focus and emphasis in the statements they have made about these chapters reveal both this common concern and their own special interests and experience.

What did these educators identify as the major crisis in the schools? Burton P. Fowler, for thirteen years the chairman of the Committee on School and College Relations of the Educational Records Bureau, and the prime mover of this study, has cited it in the Foreword: "The gap between learning in school and responsible social action both in and out of school remains to be bridged. *The purposes of the teachers and the purposes of the learners are often miles apart.*" Mr. Eldridge, the incoming chairman, reinforces this idea:

One of the things which impresses me here is the disparity between what these young people are yearning for or even groping for and what the school is giving them. At the risk of adding to the danger of making "values" a

151

hackneyed word, I should like to suggest that this element in a school experience seems to be generally ignored or avoided, whereas it should be made transcendent. Even if one accepts the principle that high school is primarily a place for acquiring or imparting knowledge, surely the development of moral, ethical, spiritual wisdom should be a part of the process, and not submerged by the "minutiae of yesterday's exercises and tomorrow's corrections."

The disparity mentioned here appears in a different context in Eugene R. Smith's comments on a draft of this report:

If it is granted, as I believe it must be, that a most important part of the school's objectives is to try to see that every boy or girl who has attended it will leave it with more constructive ideals and purposes than those with which he or she entered, then a good deal of the material you are reporting here must be considered very seriously for the light it throws on our schools.

In spite of the valuable and constructive thought reflected in your quotations from many of the boys and girls, the total picture seems to me to show that schools are *not* keeping minds intent, interest high, intelligence eagerly exploring, social concern and responsibility developing. You show some situations where these are achieved, but what room for improvement!

. . . the most valuable mental training and the development of constructive values go practically hand in hand; the conditions and methods that develop mental efficiency can also develop a sense of values and *vice versa*. And what thoughtful teacher can possibly evade the responsibility for both? Are we really so obsessed with covering a text book or a laid-out course and with reaching high marks (of doubtful accuracy in any case) that our chief objectives are in serious danger? To many of the young people interviewed, it seems that we are.

The rationale for "sacrificing learning for marks" and using advanced sections for information stuffing often seems to be that admission to a prestige college demands this sort of thing. Is this realistic? Does it actually and accurately reflect the demands of the colleges? Another member of the steering committee, Eugene S. Wilson, dean of admissions at Amherst College, wrote this emphatic note on a draft of the chapter which bears directly on this problem:

This tension is real around New York City, Philadelphia, Cleveland, Chicago—in wealthy suburban areas—but not in most of the country yet.

Good teachers can promote thought and inquiry. Ironically, the most competitive colleges are paying less and less attention in selection to marks, test scores, and activities and are looking for qualities of imagination, industry, dedication—real achievement over and beyond the assigned.

If marks and the college admissions hurdle do *not* provide focus for a school program, what does? I have been haunted by one boy's comment about "waiting around to grow up" and wishing for "something more." The "something more" was unquestionably the opportunity to bear genuine responsibility in life within the school and outside. At the various schools the topic of responsibility burst through with eager descriptions when the students felt that their obligations went beyond doing the assignment and keeping out of trouble. Interestingly enough, where a school offered its students little challenge in the way of responsibility the subject was quickly dismissed, or did not come up at all.

Students could, and did, attack a course or an approach to teaching which seemed barren or meaningless to them as people. Some students hoped, even assumed, that learning could be a stimulating adventure. This is encouraging. But students who had not encountered a chance to face important responsibility either in school or in the community seemed to assume that "this was the way it had to be." They might have been astonished and encouraged to hear some of the discussions among students who had met a real test of their ability to shoulder responsibilities. Another professional on our panel, Chester F. Protheroe of Needham High School, in Massachusetts, was outspoken on this matter:

Responsibility should be genuine, not pseudo or rigged. The administrators' desire to have a smooth-running school often leads to autocracy, with the student council being given only routine motions to go through. Or—just as bad—suggestions are made by teachers, which have all the force of directives and impose upon student leaders the responsibility of taking them to the student body and getting them carried out.

What I would like to see is the opportunity for students to make decisions for their own governance. If they turn out to be unwise decisions, the youngsters will learn to avoid repeating them. I very much doubt that a school permitting this will become an utter shambles, and it would certainly turn out better citizens than does the spoon-fed kind of school.

The climate of the school is, after all, a matter of the conviction of the people responsible. Esther Raushenbush of Sarah Lawrence College points out that

... we can monkey all we want to with devices and curriculum changes, debate about what is a good size for a school, or whether college-bound and non-college-bound students belong together, or how advanced placement classes should be handled, but what counts is the climate of the institution and the values it has, and instills, not by a program, but by its existence. Programs help, obviously, but these are consequences of a climate, not the primary causes of it. It is an attitude toward education which produces activities related to the UN, not *vice versa*. I think it is healthy to deal with this fact: what gives a school the kind of influence over its students that some of these schools have is the conviction the people who *make* the school have about education and about students.

Robert D. North, associate director of the Educational Records Bureau, the organization which sponsored this study, made this statement on reading the final draft of the report:

Research-minded readers may be disturbed to find that this study did not begin with definitions of terms, a well-formulated research design, or provisions for objective evaluation. In planning this study, the committee felt that much would be lost and little gained if an attempt were made to fit the material into pre-cast molds. What has emerged, therefore, is not neatly structured, but neither is it completely amorphous or ambiguous.

The findings are a mosaic, highlighted by the revelation that alert, reflective, humanitarian-minded youngsters are *very much in evidence* in our public and private secondary schools.

Perhaps the study director just happened to get an off-beat sample of the so-called "silent, apathetic, security-minded generation." While possible, this seems unlikely. Perhaps, instead, the younger generation has been misrepresented in some of the other studies, or it may now be in a transitional stage. If so, the implications of the findings are far-reaching for those who have the responsibility for providing instruction and guidance for this generation of secondary school students.

THE STUDY DIRECTOR'S PERSPECTIVE

Over and over again I wished for this or that commentator, armchair educator, or viewer-with-alarm-of-the-young, to be invisibly present in the room while these students were talking. The facile way so many people underestimate the potential thoughtfulness, constructiveness, and maturity of vision of high school students is sharply challenged by a great deal of what I have heard and saw and have tried to report. I have heard that high-school-age people are anti-adult, cynical, sliders-by; that they are anti-intellectual, and reflect the worst in our culture. I can say only that I have encountered several hundred young people who had none of these traits. And I do not believe that the eight schools we selected so carefully are so far removed from the flow of American life that they "don't count."

STUDENTS' APPROACH TO THE STUDY

I was consistently struck by the interest the students took in discussing the idea of "the impact of the school on the students as people." The word "values" seemed forbidding to some, sanctimonious to others, interesting to still others. But the idea of a concern for students as human beings seemed something to be taken seriously in literally every discussion. No other explanation can account for the intensity and eagerness so many students showed in exploring their school experiences. I did not encounter a single group or even an individual who seemed to take a superficial or casual attitude toward the subject of this study. Even at their most critical moments, students were careful, it seemed to me, to be fair and to avoid pettiness and griping.

The comments that I heard most often about the discussions themselves was, "This was good. We ought to do more of this." Such reactions continually made clear to me that these students liked trying to get some perspective on their school experience and felt the need for attaining it.

These young people were eager to question each other. They might have felt a need to present a united front on certain subjects, but generally they provided some of the liveliest and most revealing material for this report when they were challenging each other, "across"—rather than through—the questioner. Seriousness and thoughtfulness in approaching the concerns of this study were every bit as evident among vocational, general, and business students as among college preparatory and advanced standing students. Their concerns varied, as the report shows, but they all recognized the importance of the school's impact on its students as people.

CONFORMITY AND INDIVIDUALITY

The more sophisticated the students, the more hostility they showed toward the idea of a deadening, stifling conformity. For many of them this was no parlor *cliché*, but a battle cry. The willingness of so many students to make extreme statements within the hearing of their classmates indicates that this *verbal* objection to certain kinds of conformity was supported by a good deal of courage in action. It might be claimed that the discussions were centered on topics that were not private enough or sufficiently emotionally charged to provide a real test of moral courage. I do not believe this was true. Many of these students had read or heard about reports characterizing the whole generation as self-centered and security-minded, searching for faceless conformity. The students with whom I talked were infuriated by such stereotypes. They were willing to stand up and be counted for their convictions.

AN IMPRESSION OF THE STUDENTS

If I were to try to put into capsule form an over-all impression of the high school students I met and listened to—their attitudes, beliefs, sense of values, and reactions to their school and community—I would say this: Contrary to much popular opinion about teen-agers, these students are not anti-adult or anti-intellectual. Neither are they cynical nor apathetic.

They criticized courses that stressed routine learning, memorizing, and busy-work. They especially criticized the idea that such activities are necessary components of education.

Many of the students were preparing for college, and they recognized that the drive for admission to prestige colleges was an overriding motive in their school lives. Yet they felt that the striving for high marks and outstanding test scores was not enough. They were seeking a purpose in their school life: in their courses, in their responsibilities, in their activities. They spoke out for a challenge to think, to explore, and to come to grips with their work in each subject in some kind of personal, meaningful way. There was no overriding desire from students for full responsibility in running their schools. They were willing and eager to benefit from informed adult guidance. Nevertheless, they regarded increased responsibility and increased independence as crucial to their own maturation during their high school years.

The students speaking out in this report would probably be the first to challenge the statement I have just made. They were critical of studies and articles that generalized from small amounts of data and that labeled high school students in some convenient way. And, of course, the *differences* among students' experiences and attitudes, as this report shows, are of great significance: differences in attitudes toward students of different educational aims, abilities, or social backgrounds; differences in the kind of private or mutual philosophical exploration they were doing; differences in their *experience* of personal challenge in and out of classrooms. Thus, even as I try to make a capsule statement, I am thrown back to the *diversity* which I heard and have tried to report. The boy was right who said, "They talk about us as if teen-agers were all alike. But we're *not* all alike and somebody'd better get this idea pretty soon."

BEYOND GENERALIZATIONS

Generalizations often blur the outline of the specifics. Words about thoughtfulness, maturity, potentiality, interest, courtesy, diversity, and friendliness are useful only as quick substitutes for the students' actual words quoted here in the report. In spite of generalizations, the hundreds of young people who spoke out are still individuals. Who are they? They are the electricity student who had found something he really liked; the boy from the lumber camps who found in athletics a way to break down social barriers; the girl who was surprised to find that she was not the only one in her school who was concerned about God and ethics and meaning; the merit scholarship winner who cried out, "You have to sacrifice learning for marks!"; the "shop kid" who was grateful for the ban on dungarees so "we can get to look like the college prep kids;" the girl who explained how her school "was like a very good democracy— you feel you have a place;" and the boy who felt that school had enabled him "to know myself better."

In a report centered on *students* speaking about their experiences in school, surely even this section on perspectives should end with a word from the students. I think of the boy who wanted to warn me against "asking the bull questions." Most of all, another statement he made reminds us that we have in our schools a wealth of what is often so coldly called "human resources": "You'll find that when the chips are down the people will come through pretty well in this school. They don't talk like much, but there are times when they *do* pretty well!"

CHAPTER 26
ECHOES IN THE EMPTY HALL

Where do you stand now at the end of this study? It isn't a matter of writing down hard and fast generalizations. It is something like the last look down the hall of a school before you close the door, with your memories of voices echoing there in the hall. Which words echo loudest?—
AGATHA TOWNSEND, MEMBER OF THE STEERING COMMITTEE OF THIS STUDY, AUTHOR OF *College Freshmen Speak Out.**

Out of the experience of talking with these students, out of the writing of this report and listening to the echoes of all the voices I heard speaking out about the high school experience, one strong conviction has emerged. I would hope that the students' words would leave different impressions with different readers of this report. I do not see how any two readers could respond in just the same way to it. Even so, I cannot end the report without taking the opportunity to say "where I stand now" in relation to all I heard—about curriculum and teaching, college admission, responsibility, divisive forces in school and developing values. The conviction I have reached is this: *The school must give the student an intellectual challenge to come into action as a sensitive, thinking, feeling individual.*

At the heart of this conviction is a more extended and inclusive meaning of "intellectual challenge" than is apparent in much of the current debate about "the trouble with our schools." "Intellectual challenge" is commonly used nowadays to stand for tripled homework, rigid ability sectioning, fixed requirements for all, preoccupation with the gifted student, intensive drilling in facts and concepts. None of these *necessarily* develops or even stimulates critical thinking, or leads to student understanding of the structure and operations of a subject. Nor do they *necessarily* meet the needs of the human being who comes each

* Agatha Townsend, *College Freshmen Speak Out.* New York: Harper & Brothers, 1956.

159

morning to school. These conclusions seem to be warranted by the experiences described in this study.

What is genuine intellectual challenge? It is what the boy was searching for when he said, "I haven't had a chance in any course to really think. They tell us you go to school to widen your understanding and all, but where are you supposed to do it?"

Perhaps such students are struggling with two problems at once. One is that they cannot find any relation between what they are studying and what they feel, care about, and see as real. The other is that they cannot see the actual design, the "workings" of a given intellectual discipline. Exhortation to the young to *make an effort* does not help in meeting either of these problems. This is true particularly because of the major effort so many of these students were already making anyway, for points, marks, records, and the rest. The solution for each of these two problems rests as much or more in the hands of curriculum planners and teachers as in those of students.

"HOW IT RELATES TO ME . . ."

Psychologists tell us that much of an adolescent's experience seems distant and unreal to him. Endless descriptions have been written of the inner life of the teen-ager. It is easier to plan a curriculum, a course, or a lesson if the planner ignores all this information. "We are not psychologists," teachers and curriculum planners can say, "and, anyway, teen-age fads change. What we have that is constant is *the subject.*" This is a tempting road to take, but all too often it allows the planner and teacher to disregard the experiences and visions which the students bring to school every morning and which could be used to enliven the subject, to give it a new dimension of genuine relevance for the learners.

In other words, the current interest in giving students more challenging work could be a magnificent new beginning. Clearly, however, it can run into the pitfall of more work without more thought, more time looking at print without more intellectual exploration. Courses and curricula demanding more work can be planned and "put over." Abundant weapons are on hand for putting them over: pressures of marks, college admission, parent and teacher approval, job recommendations, and all the rest. Such pressures can put over just about any course, regardless of the students' interest in it *per se*. But are we satisfied if the results develop only a number of brilliant, shrewd, test-takers and scholarship winners? Remember the boy who said, ". . . most people around here figure it's the score you end up with that counts. They figure that after you graduate, the high school experience will seem pretty insignificant."

If we really care about the gifted students we discuss so animatedly these days, then how can we greet them with doubled work loads of highly uniform pattern? If we are serious about education in a democracy, then how can we settle for uniform dullness for the "average" student? Planning that classifies students and then "takes care" of each classification *regardless of the people in it* can hardly claim to nurture individual creativity, the courageous leap of a penetrating mind, or even the feeling that thinking is worth a person's effort.

No one is asking that the school give over hours so students can tell the story of their lives, hopes, and dreams. Many of the students who were most critical of courses that were remote and unrelated to them were quickest to object to irrelevancy in the sense of "going off on a tangent." Basically the relevance to the human community of literature, science, language, composition, the arts, history, and related subjects surely is not even debatable. How is it, then, that students—and teachers—so often miss this relevance? Why would a bright, reasonably cooperative senior girl talk about the need for "bridges to 'out there,'" for something "less unreal" than the supposedly high-powered program she encountered all day in school?

WAYS THE RELEVANCE GETS LOST

One answer is that teachers and students may be submerged in minutiae. Another is what one boy called his school's "neurotic obsession" with grades, test scores, and prestige colleges when this obsession takes over the intellectual life. Other answers point to the competition that anything inside the classroom faces from the intensities outside where life always seems more real. Yet all these answers may obscure a simple one that deserves some notice: it is a long journey from the essential design of a subject, through the curriculum, textbooks, and lesson plans, to the student. On this journey it is easy for the subject to lose its challenge for the student who comes, so often hopefully, to meet it.

I stress this idea of the student's hopes for a course because even the most critical young people I heard seemed to assume that there could or should be "something for me," "something alive," in a school course. I value this hopefulness highly. It is in glad contrast to what I heard from one boy who was in a group of college students to whom I had been talking about some of the findings of this study. This college junior said, "A lot of us have a feeling that those kids' hopes for the curriculum were kind of pathetic. They seemed really to believe that you could get something living and personal in a course. We've pretty much figured you can't. We've long since given up that hope and have looked somewhere else for this 'meaning.' " For this particular group of college students, the "somewhere else" was in their own social and political interests and activities. This was fortunate for them and for the community. Yet, to me, this attitude of theirs seemed pathetic. They had become resigned to thinking that relevance and personal challenge were not to be found anywhere in academic life, but must always be sought elsewhere. By contrast, the high school students had not completely surrendered to apathy.

SHEEP AND GOATS

This plea, for something that presents a challenge in a personal and meaningful way, came not only from college-bound students but from those in business, vocational, and general programs as well. Descriptions of what this challenge was like when it was present also came from students in all kinds of programs. Remember the boys in the vocational drawing class who explained their appreciation for activity "where we're really learning something," and who had developed a sense of personal achievement. There was also the girl in the general program who said that many things in history really meant a lot more to her "because I could explore them and think about them, and not have to think about them just as something I had to be marked on to get into college." We could cite the teacher talking about the effect on his student of playing the lead in *The Crucible*; or the discussion of the memorable English course—which one girl said she wouldn't have missed "even though I never got to Elizabethan literature," and many others. These students welcomed the opportunity to think and grow as people. If they did not find it in their school, they were disappointed, even angry. Even the students in the class that felt school "had no business influencing you" were soon eagerly discussing school experiences that did have an impact on their lives.

THOUGHT AND NON-THOUGHT

"Teach fundamentals—thinking comes later!" This view is popular among college teachers who tell high school teachers what to do. "We'll teach them to think!" The argument of the college teacher continues, "You give them the tools, something to think about." The fact is that thinking is going on vigorously at all stages, whether or not it is promoted in the classroom. When it is invited and rewarded in the classroom, the results can be electrifying. I wonder about the value of any drill on tools or "fundamentals" which does not fit into some intelligible design, both in a subject's nature and in the student's understanding. I have heard this matter heatedly discussed. These who see high school as an experience in mental calesthenics, to which meaning will be given in the future, would be horrified if they stood in a classroom among students who felt that this was their lot.

The kind of relevance students wanted, and appreciated when they found it, is related to "fundamentals." That term, like "intellectual challenge," needs elucidation. Articulate students clearly explained that fundamental learning, to them, means much more than drawing parallels to personal experience. They said it was not a matter of relating the study of *Macbeth* to "the way you felt when your ambition pushed you so hard to be football captain." Instead, it is a matter of seeing some point, some design, of making some discovery oneself, in learning and living simultaneously. Too often students are asked to learn the names of things, the descriptions of processes, even what are called "interpretations," without being given an opportunity to develop for themselves a sense of what the things, the processes, the matters interpreted *are*. As one student said, "Everything's all known and worked out. Even the teacher's course is all finished. There's nothing for *us* to do but learn the answers and agree."

Jerome S. Bruner, a Harvard psychologist, writes, in *The Process of Education**:

There has been much written on the role of reward and punishment in learning, but very little indeed on the role of interest and curiosity and the lure of discovery. If it is our intention as teachers to inure the child to longer and longer episodes of learning, it may well be that intrinsic rewards in the form of quickened awareness and understanding will have to be emphasized far more in the detailed design of curricula. One of the least-discussed ways of carrying a student through a hard unit of material is to challenge him with a chance to exercise his full powers, so that he may discover the pleasure of full and effective functioning. Good teachers know the power of this lure. Students should know what it feels like to be completely absorbed in a problem. They seldom experience this feeling in school.

In this book, Dr. Bruner calls attention to the research that is going on at the frontiers of each of the major academic fields. He explains that the biologists, mathematicians, historians, and others who are doing this research have a view of their respective fields that is similar in some ways to the perspective of the first-grade child, for whom all academic knowledge is a frontier. The scholar at the forefront of his discipline, however, is generally aware of the relation between his advanced work and the "structure of his subject," as Dr. Bruner puts it. If a pupil, from the first grade on, could be helped to recognize the relation between his school work and man's continuing struggle to amass knowledge, school learning could become a more relevant and meaningful experience for the individual. This type of educational process might well replace the "drill now, think later," approach to school study—an approach which ignores both the student as a person and the subject as a structure.

WHEN THERE IS RELEVANCE

What creates "relevance?" Does it need to be "created" if, as we have just suggested, it is already in the subject itself—if our students could only get at it? I doubt if there is a prescription for achieving relevance,

* Jerome S. Bruner, *The Process of Education*. Cambridge: Harvard University Press, 1960.

but I believe I have seen and heard students who recognized it and treasured it. I saw it through the eyes of the boy who said, ". . . we feel that there's some place for the things we're personally interested in, even though we study a number of things together. . . ."

I believe relevance was the keynote for the advanced history class that was so insistent on the idea of individual responsibility; for the mathematics class that was so enthusiastic about developing a textbook; for the boy in the cafeteria who was trying to explain how his history course "helped the pieces to add up to something." I think it was recognized by the physics student who was so grateful for the period when "possibilities" were discussed in "the things we needed to explore in this century."

I am perhaps most haunted by the echo of two comments I heard early in the study. The first was the boy's off-hand dismissal of his courses: "curriculum is curriculum . . . we haven't mentioned it because we wanted to tell you first about the things that really matter." The second bears even more directly on the idea that the school must be relevant to the life and understanding of the person encountering it. It came from the girl who was talking about how easy it is to evade the big questions and concerns: "You plunge into trivialities . . . at school you can just keep busy. At home there's homework. . . ." Surely the school should offer the students a challenge that goes further than just providing them with an escape from preoccupations or inundating them with busywork. It could, in its entirety, be what one course was for the boy who said, "It's the kind of thing that makes you take a new look at the world around you."

INDEX

169